A Little
Night Music

A Little Night Music.

A NEW MUSICAL COMEDY

Book by Hugh Wheeler

Music and Lyrics by Stephen Sondheim

Suggested by a Film by Ingmar Bergman

❁

Originally Produced and Directed on Broadway

by Harold Prince

Illustrated with a drawing by Al Hirschfeld

and photographs

DODD, MEAD & COMPANY
NEW YORK

CAUTION: Professionals and amateurs are hereby warned that *A Little Night Music,* being fully protected under the Copyright Laws of the United States of America and all other countries of the Berne and Universal Copyright Conventions, is subject to royalty. All rights, including but not limited to, professional, amateur, recording, motion picture, recitation, lecturing, public reading, radio and television broadcasting, and the rights of translation into foreign languages are strictly reserved, permission for which must be secured in writing from the Authors' agents, Flora Roberts, Inc. (for Stephen Sondheim and Harold S. Prince) 116 East 59th Street, New York, New York 10022 and William Morris Agency, Inc. (for Hugh Wheeler), att: Jerome Talbert, 1350 Avenue of the Americas, New York, New York 10019.

Printed in the United States of America

A Little Night Music was first presented by Harold Prince in association with Ruth Mitchell at the Shubert Theatre, New York City, on February 25, 1973.

ORIGINAL BROADWAY CAST

(in order of appearance)

Mr. Lindquist	BENJAMIN RAYSON
Mrs. Nordstrom	TERI RALSTON
Mrs. Anderssen	BARBARA LANG
Mr. Erlansen	GENE VARRONE
Mrs. Segstrom	BETH FOWLER
Fredrika Armfeldt	JUDY KAHAN
Madame Armfeldt	HERMIONE GINGOLD
Frid, her butler	GEORGE LEE ANDREWS
Henrik Egerman	MARK LAMBERT
Anne Egerman	VICTORIA MALLORY
Fredrik Egerman	LEN CARIOU
Petra	D. JAMIN-BARTLETT
Desiree Armfeldt	GLYNIS JOHNS
Malla, her maid	DESPO
Bertrand, a page	WILL SHARPE MARSHALL
Count Carl-Magnus Malcolm	LAURENCE GUITTARD
Countess Charlotte Malcolm	PATRICIA ELLIOTT
Osa	SHERRY MATHIS

VICTORIA MALLORY, GARN STEPHENS (REPLACED PRIOR TO THE BROADWAY OPENING BY D. JAMIN-BARTLETT), GEORGE LEE ANDREWS, LAURENCE GUITTARD, PATRICIA ELLIOTT, LEN CARIOU, GLYNNIS JOHNS AND HERMIONE GINGOLD IN "A LITTLE NIGHT MUSIC"

Before the houselights are down, MR. LINDQUIST *appears and sits at the piano. He removes his gloves, plunks a key, and begins to vocalize.* MRS. NORDSTROM *enters, hits a key on the piano, and vocalizes with him.* MRS. ANDERSSEN, MR. ERLANSEN *and* MRS. SEGSTROM *come out and join the vocalizing.*

MEN	GIRLS
La, La La La	La, La La La
La, La La La	La, La La La

MRS. NORDSTROM
The old deserted beach that we walked—
Remember?

MR. ERLANSEN
Remember?
The cafe in the park where we talked—
Remember?

1

A LITTLE NIGHT MUSIC

MRS. ANDERSSEN
 Remember?
 The tenor on the boat that we chartered,
 Belching "The Bartered Bride"—

ALL
 Ah, how we laughed,
 Ah, how we cried,

MR. LINDQUIST	GIRLS and MEN
Ah, how you promised	La, La La La
And	
Ah, how	Ah . . .
I lied.	Lie . . . lie . . . lie . . .

MRS. SEGSTROM
 That dilapidated inn—
 Remember, darling?

MR. ERLANSEN
 The proprietress' grin,
 Also her glare.

MRS. NORDSTROM
 Yellow gingham on the bed—
 Remember, darling?

MR. LINDQUIST
 And the canopy in red,
 Needing repair

2

ALL

Soon, I promise.
Soon I won't shy away,
Dear old—
Soon. I want to.
Soon, whatever you say.
Even

GIRLS	MEN
Now	Now, when we touch,
When we're close and	
We	
Touch	Touching my brow,
And you're kissing my	
Brow,	Ahhhh . . .
I don't mind it	
Too much.	
And you'll have to	

ALL

Admit I'm endearing,
I help keep things humming,
I'm not domineering,
What's one small shortcoming?

And

Unpack the luggage, La La La
Pack up the luggage, La La La
Unpack the luggage, La La La
Hi-ho, the glamorous life!

3

A LITTLE NIGHT MUSIC

Unpack the luggage, La La La
Pack up the luggage, La La La
Unpack the luggage, La La La
Hi-ho, the glamorous life!

MR. LINDQUIST	OTHERS MEMBERS OF QUINTET
Ahhhhh . . .	Unpack the luggage, La La La
	Pack up the luggage, La La La

MRS. NORDSTROM	OTHER MEMBERS OF THE QUINTET
Ahhhh . . .	Unpack the luggage, La La La
	Hi-ho, the glamorous life!

ALL
Bring up the curtain, La La La
Bring down the curtain, La La La
Bring up the curtain, La La La

ALL
Hi-ho, hi-ho
For the glamorous life!

(*After the applause, the* QUINTET *starts to waltz. The show curtain flies out, revealing the* MAIN CHARACTERS *doing a strangely surreal waltz of their own, in which partners change partners and recouple with others. The* QUINTET *drifts up into the waltzing* COUPLES, *and reappears to hum accompaniment for the last section of the dance.* FREDRIKA *wanders through the waltz, too, watching*)

ACT I

Prologue

At the end of the Opening Waltz, MADAME ARMFELDT *is brought on in her wheelchair by her butler,* FRID. *In her lap is a tray containing a silver cigarette box, a small vase with four yellow bud-roses, and the cards with which she is playing solitaire. She is watched by* FREDRIKA ARMFELDT, *13—a grave, very self-contained and formal girl with the precise diction of the convent-trained.*

FREDRIKA If you cheated a little, it would come out.

MADAME ARMFELDT (*continuing to play*) Solitaire is the only thing in life that demands absolute honesty. As a woman who has numbered kings among her lovers, I think my word can be taken on that point.

(*She motions to* FRID, *who crosses down and lights her cigarette*)

What was I talking about?

FREDRIKA You said I should watch.

MADAME ARMFELDT Watch—what?

5

FREDRIKA It sounds very unlikely to me, but you said I should watch for the night to smile.

MADAME ARMFELDT Everything is unlikely, dear, so don't let that deter you. Of course the summer night smiles. Three times.

FREDRIKA But how does it smile?

MADAME ARMFELDT Good heavens, what sort of a nanny did you have?

FREDRIKA None, really. Except Mother, and the other actresses in the company—and the stage manager.

MADAME ARMFELDT Stage managers are not nannies. They don't have the talent.

FREDRIKA But if it happens—how does it happen?

MADAME ARMFELDT You get a feeling. Suddenly the jasmine starts to smell stronger, then a frog croaks—then all the stars in Orion wink. Don't squeeze your bosoms against the chair, dear. It'll stunt their growth. And then where would you be?

FREDRIKA But why does it smile, Grandmother?

6

MADAME ARMFELDT   At the follies of human beings, of course. The first smile smiles at the young, who know nothing.

(*She looks pointedly at* FREDRIKA)

The second, at the fools who know too little, like Desiree.

FREDRIKA   Mother isn't a fool.

MADAME ARMFELDT (*Going right on*)   Um hum. And the third at the old who know too much—like me.

(*The game is over without coming out. Annoyed at the cards,* MADAME ARMFELDT *scatters them at random, and barks at* FRID)

Frid, time for my nap.

FREDRIKA (*Intrigued in spite of herself, gazes out at the summer night*)   Grandmother, might it really smile tonight?

MADAME ARMFELDT   Why not? Now, practice your piano, dear, preferably with the soft pedal down. And as a treat tonight at dinner, I shall tell you amusing stories about my liaison with the Baron de Signac, who was, to put it mildly, peculiar.

(FRID *wheels her off and* FREDRIKA *goes to sit at the piano*)

ACT I
Scene 1

THE EGERMAN ROOMS

Two rooms: the parlor and the master bedroom, in-dicated on different levels. ANNE EGERMAN, *a ravishingly pretty girl of 18, is on the bed. She goes to the vanity table, toys with her hair, and then enters the parlor.* HENRIK EGERMAN, *her stepson, a brooding young man of 19, is seated on the sofa, playing his cello. Beside him on the sofa is a book with a ribbon marker.* ANNE *looks at* HENRIK, *then leans over the sofa to get his attention.*

ANNE   Oh Henrik, dear, don't you have anything less gloomy to practice?

HENRIK   It isn't gloomy, it's profound.

ANNE (*Reaches down, takes* HENRIK'S *book, and begins reading from it*)   ". . . in discussing temptation, Martin Luther says: 'You cannot prevent the birds from flying over your head, but you can prevent them from nesting in your hair.'" Oh dear, that's gloomy too! Don't they teach you anything at the seminary a little more cheerful?

HENRIK (*Grand*)   A man who's going to serve in God's Army must learn all the ruses and stratagems of the Enemy.

ANNE (*Giggling*)   And which of your professors made that historic statement?

HENRIK (*Caught out*)   Pastor Ericson, as a matter of fact. He says we're like generals learning to win battles against the devil.

(*Her ball of silk falls off her lap*)

ANNE   Oh dear, my ball!

(HENRIK *bends down to pick up the ball. He stands beside her, obviously overwhelmed by her nearness.* ANNE *pats her lap*)

You can put it there, you know. My lap isn't one of the Devil's snares.

(*Flushing,* HENRIK *drops the ball into her lap and moves away from her*)

HENRIK   Anne, I was wondering—could we go for a walk?

ANNE   Now?

HENRIK   I've so much to tell you. What I've been thinking, and everything.

ANNE   Silly Henrik, don't you realize it's almost tea-time?
And I think I hear your father.

(*She rises, puts down the ball of silk*)

I'm sure you've made the most wonderful discoveries about
life, and I long to talk, but—later.

(FREDRIK *enters, followed by* PETRA)

Fredrik dear!

HENRIK (*Mutters to himself*)   Later.

ANNE   Look who's come home to us—holier than ever.

FREDRIK   Hello, son. How was the examination?

HENRIK   Well, as a matter of fact . . .

FREDRIK (*Breaking in*)   You passed with flying colors, of
course.

ANNE   First on the list.

HENRIK (*Trying again*)   And Pastor Ericson said . . .

FREDRIK (*Breaking in*)   Splendid—you must give us a full
report. Later.

ANNE   He'd better be careful or he'll go straight to heaven
before he has a chance to save any sinners.

10

FREDRIK   Don't tease him, dear.

ANNE   Oh, Henrik likes to be teased, don't you, Henrik? Fredrik, do you want your tea now?

FREDRIK   Not now, I think. It's been rather an exhausting day in Court and as we have a long evening ahead of us, I feel a little nap is indicated.

   (*He produces theater tickets from his pocket*)

ANNE   (*Grabbing at them, delighted as a child*)   Tickets for the theater!

FREDRIK   It's a French comedy. I thought it might entertain you.

ANNE   It's "Woman Of The World," isn't it? With Desiree Armfeldt! She's on all the posters! Oh, Fredrik, how delicious!

   (*To* HENRIK, *teasing*)

What shall I wear? My blue with the feathers—

   (FREDRIK *pours water*)

genuine angel's feathers—? Or the yellow? Ah, I know. My pink, with the bosom. And Henrik, you can do me up in the back.

   (*She goes into the bedroom*)

FREDRIK   I'm sorry, son. I should have remembered you were coming home and got a third ticket. But then perhaps a French comedy is hardly suitable.

(FREDRIK *takes a pill*)

HENRIK (*Outburst*)   Why does everyone laugh at me? Is it so ridiculous to want to do some good in this world?

FREDRIK   I'm afraid being young in itself can be a trifle ridiculous. Good has to be so good, bad so bad. Such superlatives!

HENRIK   But to be old, I suppose, is not ridiculous.

FREDRIK (*Sigh*)   Ah, let's not get into that. I love you very much, you know. So does Anne—in her way. But you can't expect her to take your mother's place. She's young too; she has not yet learned . . .

HENRIK   . . . to suffer fools gladly?

FREDRIK (*Gentle*)   You said that, son. Not I.

ANNE   Fredrik!

(*As* FREDRIK *moves into the bedroom,* HENRIK *picks up his book and reads.* ANNE *is buffing her nails*)

You were sweet to think of the theater for me.

FREDRIK   I'll enjoy it too.

12

ANNE   Who wouldn't—when all the posters call her The One
And Only Desiree Armfeldt?

(FREDRIK *begins to try to kiss her. She rattles on*)

I wonder what it would feel like to be a One and Only! The
One and Only—Anne Egerman!

(*She leaves* FREDRIK *on the bed and moves to the vanity
table. As aware as he is of her rejection*)

Poor Fredrik! Do I still make you happy? After eleven
months? I know I'm foolish to be so afraid—and you've
been so patient, but, soon—I promise. Oh, I know you think
I'm too silly to worry, but I do . . .

(*As* FREDRIK *looks up to answer, she gives a little cry*)

Oh no! For heaven's sakes, can that be a pimple coming?

(FREDRIK, *deflated, begins to sing*)

FREDRIK (*Singing*)
Now, as the sweet imbecilities
Tumble so lavishly
Onto her lap . . .

ANNE   Oh Fredrik, what a day it's been! Unending drama!
While Petra was brushing my hair, the doorbell . . .

13

A LITTLE NIGHT MUSIC

FREDRIK
　Now, there are two possibilities:
　A, I could ravish her,
　B, I could nap.

ANNE　. . . that grumpy old Mrs. Nordstrom from next door.
　Her sister's coming for a visit.

FREDRIK
　Say it's the ravishment, then we see
　The option
　That follows, of course:

ANNE　. . . do hope I'm imperious enough with the servants.
　I try to be. But half the time I think they're laughing at me.

FREDRIK
　A, the deployment of charm, or B,
　The adoption
　Of physical force.

　　(*Music*)

　Now B might arouse her,
　But if I assume
　I trip on my trouser
　Leg crossing the room . . .

　　(*Music*)

　Her hair getting tangled,
　Her stays getting snapped,

My nerves will be jangled,
My energy sapped . . .

(*Music*)

Removing her clothing
Would take me all day
And her subsequent loathing
Would turn me away—
Which eliminates B
And which leaves us with A.

ANNE   Could you ever be jealous of me?

FREDRIK
Now, insofar as approaching it,
What would be festive
But have its effect?

ANNE   Shall I learn Italian? I think it would be amusing, if the verbs aren't too irregular.

FREDRIK
Now, there are two ways of broaching it:
A, the suggestive
And B, the direct.

ANNE   . . . but then French is a much chic-er language. Everyone says so. Parlez-vous Français?

A LITTLE NIGHT MUSIC

≼

FREDRIK
Say that I settle on B, to wit,
A charmingly
Lecherous mood . . .

(*Music*)

A, I could put on my nightshirt or sit
Disarmingly,
B, in the nude . . .

(*Music*)

That might be effective,
My body's all right—
But not in perspective
And not in the light . . .

(*Music*)

I'm bound to be chilly
And feel a buffoon,
But nightshirts are silly
In midafternoon . . .

(*Music*)

Which leaves the suggestive,
But how to proceed?

Although she gets restive,
Perhaps I could read . . .

(*Music*)

In view of her penchant
For something romantic,
De Sade is too trenchant
And Dickens too frantic,
And Stendhal would ruin
The plan of attack,
As there isn't much blue in
"The Red and the Black."

(*Music*)

De Maupassant's candor
Would cause her dismay.
The Brontës are grander
But not very gay.
Her taste is much blander,
I'm sorry to say,
But is Hans Christian Ander-
Sen ever risque?
Which eliminates A.

(*Exits upstage*)

ANNE   And he said, "You're such a pretty lady!" Wasn't that
silly?

FREDRIK   (*As he walks back on*)
  Now, with my mental facilities
  Partially muddied
  And ready to snap . . .

ANNE (*At the jewel box now*)   . . . I'm sure about the brace-
  let. But earrings, earrings! *Which* earrings?

FREDRIK
  Now, though there are possibilities
  Still to be studied,
  I might as well nap . . .

ANNE   Mother's rubies? . . . Oh, the diamonds are—Agony!
  I know . . .

FREDRIK
  Bow though I must
  To adjust
  My original plan . . .

ANNE   Desiree Armfeldt—I just know she'll wear the most
  glamorous gowns!

FREDRIK
  How shall I sleep
  Half as deep
  As I usually can? . . .

ANNE   Dear, distinguished old Fredrik!

FREDRIK
When now I still want and/or love you,
Now, as always,

Now,
Anne?

> (FREDRIK *turns over and goes to sleep. They remain
> frozen.* PETRA, *21, the charming, easy-going maid, en-
> ters the parlor*)

PETRA   Nobody rang. Doesn't he want his tea?

HENRIK (*Still deep in book*)   They're taking a nap.

PETRA (*Coming up behind him, teasingly ruffling his hair*)
You smell of soap.

HENRIK (*Pulling his head away*)   I'm reading.

PETRA (*Caressing his head*)   Do those old teachers take a
scrubbing brush to you every morning and scrub you down
like a dray horse?

> (*Strokes his ear*)

HENRIK (*Fierce*)   Get away from me!

PETRA (*Jumping up in mock alarm*)   Oh what a wicked
woman I am! I'll go straight to hell!

> (*Starting away, she goes toward the door, deliberately
> wiggling her hips*)

HENRIK (*Looking up, even fiercer*)   And don't walk like that!

PETRA (*Innocent*)   Like—what?

> (*Wiggles even more*)

Like this?

HENRIK (*Pleadingly*)   Stop it. Stop it?

> (*He rises, goes after her, clutches her, and starts savagely, clumsily, to kiss her and fumble at her breasts. She slaps his hand*)

PETRA   Careful!

> (*Breaks away*)

That's a new blouse! A whole week's wages and the lace extra!

> (*Looks at him*)

Poor little Henrik!

> (*Then affectionately pats his cheek*)

Later! You'll soon get the knack of it!

> (*She exits.* HENRIK *puts down the book, gets his cello and begins to sing, accompanying himself on the cello*)

20

HENRIK
 Later . . .
 When is later? . . .
 All you ever hear is "Later, Henrik! Henrik, later . . ."
 "Yes, we know, Henrik.
 Oh, Henrik—
 Everyone agrees, Henrick—
 Please, Henrik!"
 You have a thought you're fairly bursting with,
 A personal discovery or problem, and it's
 "What's your rush, Henrik?
 Shush, Henrik—
 Goodness, how you gush, Henrik—
 Hush, Henrik!"
 You murmur,
 "I only . . .
 It's just that . . .
 For God's sake!"
 "Later, Henrik . . ."

 "Henrik" . . .
 Who is "Henrik?" . . .
 Oh, that lawyer's son, the one who mumbles—
 Short and boring,
 Yes, he's hardly worth ignoring
 And who cares if he's all dammed—

 (*Looks up*)

 —I beg your pardon—
 Up inside?
 As I've

A LITTLE NIGHT MUSIC

Often stated,
It's intolerable
Being tolerated.
"Reassure Henrik,
Poor Henrik."
"Henrik, you'll endure
Being pure, Henrik."

Though I've been born, I've never been!
How can I wait around for later?
I'll be ninety on my deathbed
And the late, or rather later,
Henrik Egerman!

Doesn't anything begin?

(ANNE, *in the bedroom, gets up from the vanity table
and stands near the bed, singing to Fredrik*)

ANNE
Soon, I promise.
Soon I won't shy away,
Dear old —

(*She bites her lip*)

Soon. I want to.
Soon, whatever you say.
Even now,
When you're close and we touch,
And you're kissing my brow,
I don't mind it too much.
And you'll have to admit

I'm endearing,
I help keep things humming,
I'm not domineering,
What's one small shortcoming?
And think of how I adore you,
Think of how much you love me.
If I were perfect for you,
Wouldn't you tire of me
Soon,
All too soon?
Dear old —

(*The sound of* HENRIK's *cello.* FREDRIK *stirs noisily in bed.* ANNE *goes into the parlor*)

Henrik! That racket! Your father's sleeping!

(*She remains, half-innocent, half-coquettish, in her negligee. For a second,* ANNE *watches him. She closes her nightgown at the neck and goes back into the bedroom*)

ANNE (*Back at the bed*)
Soon—

HENRIK
"Later" . . .

ANNE
I promise.

HENRIK
When is "later?"

(*Simultaneously*)

23

A LITTLE NIGHT MUSIC

ANNE	HENRIK
Soon	"Later, Henrik, later."
I won't shy	All you ever hear is,
Away,	"Yes, we know, Henrik, oh, Henrik,
Dear old —	Everyone agrees, Henrik, please, Henrik!"

(FREDRIK *stirs. Simultaneously*)

ANNE	HENRIK	FREDRIK
Soon.	"Later" . . .	Now,
I want to.	When is "later?"	As the sweet
Soon,	All you ever	imbecilities
	Hear is	Trip on my trou-
		ser leg,
Whatever you	"Later, Henrik,	
Say.		
		Stendahl
		eliminates
		A,
	Later."	
	As I've often	
	Stated:	But
	When?	When?
Even	Maybe	Maybe
Now,		

24

ANNE	HENRIK	FREDRIK
When you're close	Soon, soon	Later,
And we touch	I'll be ninety	
	And	
And you're kissing	Dead.	When I'm kissing
My brow,		
I don't mind it		Your brow
Too much,	I don't mind it	And I'm stroking
	Too much,	your head,
		You'll come into
		my bed.
And you'll have	Since I have to	And you have to
To admit	Admit	Admit
I'm endearing,	I find peering	I've been hearing
I help	Through life's	All those
Keep things	Gray windows	tremulous cries
Humming, I'm	Impatiently	Patiently,
Not domineering,	Not very cheering.	Not interfering
What's one small	Do I fear death?	With those
		tremulous thighs.
Shortcoming?	Let it	
And	Come to me	Come to me
Think of how	Now,	Soon,
I adore you,		
Think of how	Now,	Soon,
Much you love me.		

A LITTLE NIGHT MUSIC

ANNE	HENRIK	FREDRIK
If I were perfect	Now,	Soon,
For you,		
Wouldn't you tire	Now.	Soon.
Of me		
Later?	Come to me	Come to me
	Soon. If I'm	Soon,
	Dead,	
We will,	I can	
Later.	Wait.	Straight to me,
		never mind
	How can I	How.
We will . . .	Live until	Darling,
Soon.	Later?	Now—
		I still want and/or
	Later . . .	Love
		You,
Soon.		Now, as
	Later . . .	Always,
Soon.		Now,
		(*He does a kiss*)
		Desiree.

(ANNE *stares out, astonished, as the lights go down.*
FREDRIKA, *still at the piano, is playing scales*)

FREDRIKA (*Singing*)
   Ordinary mothers lead ordinary lives:
   Keep the house and sweep the parlor,
   Cook the meals and look exhausted.
   Ordinary mothers, like ordinary wives,

26

Fry the eggs and dry the sheets and
Try to deal with facts.

Mine acts.

    (DESIREE *sweeps on with* MALLA *in tow.* MALLA *carries a wig box, suitcase, and parasol*)

DESIREE (*Singing*)
    Darling, I miss you a lot
    But, darling, this has to be short
    As mother is getting a plaque
    From the Halsingborg Arts Council
    Amateur Theatre Group.
    Whether it's funny or not,
    I'll give you a fuller report
    The minute they carry me back
    From the Halsingborg Arts Council
    Amateur Theatre Group . . .
    Love you . . .

    (THE QUINTET *appears*)

Unpack the luggage, La La La
Pack up the luggage, La La La
Unpack the luggage, La La La
Hi-ho, the glamorous life!

MRS. SEGSTROM
    Ice in the basin, La La La

MR. ERLANSEN
    Cracks in the plaster, La La La

A LITTLE NIGHT MUSIC

MRS. ANDERSSEN
  Mice in the hallway, La La La

THE QUINTET
  Hi-ho, the glamorous life!

MEN
  Run for the carriage, La La La

WOMEN
  Wolf down the sandwich, La La La

THE QUINTET
  Which town is this one? La, La, La
  Hi-ho, the glamorous life!

(FRID *wheels* MADAME ARMFELDT *onstage*)

MADAME ARMFELDT (*Singing*)
  Ordinary daughters ameliorate their lot,
  Use their charms and choose their futures,
  Breed their children, heed their mothers.
  Ordinary daughters, which mine, I fear, is not,
  Tend each asset, spend it wisely
  While it still endures . . .

  Mine tours.

DESIREE (*Singing*)
  Mother, forgive the delay,
  My schedule is driving me wild.
  But, mother, I really must run,

I'm performing in Rottvik
And don't ask where is it, please.
How are you feeling today
And are you corrupting the child?
Don't. Mother, the minute I'm done
With performing in Rottvik,
I'll come for a visit
And argue.

MEN
　Mayors with speeches, La La La

WOMEN
　Children with posies, La La La

MEN
　Half-empty houses, La La La

ALL THE QUINTET
　Hi-ho, the glamorous life!

MRS. NORDSTROM
　Cultural lunches,

ALL THE QUINTET
　La La La

MRS. ANDERSSEN
　Dead floral tributes,

ALL THE QUINTET
　La La La

A LITTLE NIGHT MUSIC

ᴋ

MR. LINDQUIST
Ancient admirers,

ALL THE QUINTET
La La La
Hi-ho, the glamorous life!

DESIREE
Pack up the luggage, La La La!
Unpack the luggage, La La La
Mother's surviving, La La La
Leading the glamorous life!

(*Holds up a mirror*)

Cracks in the plaster, La La La
Youngish admirers, La La La
Which one was that one? La La La
Hi-ho, the glamorous life!

DESIREE and THE QUINTET
Bring up the curtain, La La La
Bring down the curtain, La La La
Bring up the curtain, La La La
Hi-ho, the glamorous . . .
Life.

STAGE OF LOCAL THEATER

The show curtain is down. Two stage boxes are visible. Sitting in one are MR. LINDQUIST, MRS. NORDSTROM, *and* MR. ERLANSEN. ANNE *and* FREDRIK *enter, and speak as they walk to their box.*

ANNE   Does she look like her pictures?

FREDRIK   Who, dear?

ANNE   Desiree Armfeldt, of course.

FREDRIK   How would I know, dear?

ANNE   (*Pause*)   I only thought . . .

FREDRIK   You only thought—what?

ANNE   Desiree is not a common name. I mean, none of your typists and things are called Desiree, are they?

FREDRIK My typists and things in descending order of importance are Miss Osa Svensen, Miss Ona Nilsson, Miss Gerda Bjornson, *and* Mrs. Amalia Lindquist.

> (A PAGE *enters, and knocks three times with the staff he is carrying. The show curtain rises revealing the stage behind it, a tatty Louis XIV "salon." For a moment it is empty. Then* TWO LADIES, *in rather shabby court costumes, enter*)

FIRST LADY (MRS. SEGSTROM) Tell me something about this remarkable Countess, Madame.

SECOND LADY (MRS. ANDERSSEN) I shall try as best I can to depict the personality of the Countess, Madame, although it is too rich in mysterious contradictions to be described in a few short moments.

FIRST LADY It is said that her power over men is most extraordinary.

SECOND LADY There is a great deal of truth in that, Madame, and her lovers are as many as the pearls in the necklace which she always wears.

FIRST LADY Your own husband, Madame, is supposed to be one of the handsomest pearls, is he not?

SECOND LADY He fell in love with the Countess on sight. She took him as a lover for three months and after that I had him back.

FIRST LADY And your marriage was crushed?

SECOND LADY On the contrary, Madame! My husband had become a tender, devoted, admirable lover, a faithful husband and an exemplary father. The Countess' lack of decency is most moral.

(THE PAGE *re-enters*)

PAGE The Countess Celimène de Francen de la Tour de Casa.

(*The* COUNTESS—DESIREE—*makes her sensational entrance. A storm of applause greets her.* FREDRIK *claps.* ANNE *does* not *as she glares at the stage.*

During the applause, DESIREE *makes a deep curtsey, during which, old pro that she is, she cases the house. Her eye falls on* FREDRIK. *She does a take and instantly all action freezes*)

MR. LINDQUIST (*Sings*)
Remember?

MRS. NORDSTROM (*Sings*)
Remember?

(MR. LINDQUIST and MRS. NORDSTORM *leave the stage box*)

MRS. NORDSTROM
The old deserted beach that we walked—
Remember?

A LITTLE NIGHT MUSIC

MR. LINDQUIST
Remember?
The cafe in the park where we talked—
Remember?

MRS. NORDSTROM
Remember?

MR. LINDQUIST
The tenor on the boat that we chartered,
Belching "The Bartered Bride"—

BOTH
Ah, how we laughed,
Ah, how we cried.

MR. LINDQUIST
Ah, how you promised and
Ah, how I lied.

MRS. NORDSTROM
That dilapidated inn—
Remember, darling?

MR. LINDQUIST
The proprietress' grin,
Also her glare . . .

MRS. NORDSTROM
Yellow gingham on the bed—
Remember, darling?

34

MR. LINDQUIST
  And the canopy in red,
  Needing repair?

BOTH
  I *think* you were there.

  (*They return to the stage box and the action continues*)

ANNE (*Fierce, to* FREDRIK)   She looked at us. Why did she
look at us?

DESIREE (*To* SECOND LADY)   Dear Madame Merville, what a
charming mischance to find you here this evening.

FREDRIK   I don't think she looked especially at us.

ANNE   She did! She   SECOND LADY   Charming, indeed, dear
peered, then she smiled.   Celimène.

SECOND LADY   May I be permitted to present my school friend
from the provinces? Madame Vilmorac—whose husband,
I'm sure, is in dire need of a little expert polishing.

FIRST LADY   Oh, dear Countess, you are all but a legend to
me. I implore you to reveal to me the secret of your success
with the hardier sex!

ANNE   She smiled at us!

  (*Grabs* FREDRIK'S *opera glasses and studies the stage*)

❧

DESIREE Dear Madame, that can be summed up in a single word—

ANNE She's ravishingly beautiful.

FREDRIK Make-up.

DESIREE —dignity.

TWO LADIES Dignity?

ANNE (*Turning on* FREDRIK) How can you be sure—if you've never seen her?

FREDRIK Hush!

DESIREE (*Playing her first-act set speech*) Dignity. We women have a right to commit any crime toward our husbands, our lovers, our sons, as long as we do not hurt their dignity. We should make men's dignity our best ally and caress it, cradle it, speak tenderly to it, and handle it as our most delightful toy. Then a man is in our hands, at our feet, or anywhere else we momentarily wish him to be.

ANNE (*Sobbing*) I want to go home!   FREDRIK Anne!

ANNE I want to go home!

FREDRIK Anne!

   (*They run off*)

THE EGERMAN ROOMS

In the parlor, PETRA, *lying on the couch, is calmly rearranging her blouse.* HENRIK, *in a storm of tension, is pulling on his trousers. On the floor beside them is a bottle of champagne and two glasses.*

HENRIK   We have sinned, and it was a complete failure!

(*Struggling with his fly buttons*)

These buttons, these insufferable buttons!

PETRA   Here dear, let me.

(*She crosses, kneels in front of him, and starts to do up the fly buttons*)

Don't you worry, little Henrik. Just let it rest a while.

(*She pats his fly*)

There. Now you put on your sweater and do a nice little quiet bit of reading.

(*She gets his sweater from the back of a chair and helps him into it.*
ANNE *enters, still crying. She sees* HENRIK *and* PETRA, *lets out a sob, and runs into the bedroom.* FREDRIK *enters.*
Perfectly calm, to FREDRIK)

My, that was a short play.

FREDRIK My wife became ill; I had to bring her home.

(*He gives* HENRIK *a look, sizing up the situation approvingly, before following* ANNE *into the bedroom*)

Anne!

(HENRIK *starts again toward* PETRA, *who avoids him*)

PETRA No, lamb. I told you. Give it a nice rest and you'll be surprised how perky it'll be by morning.

(*She wriggles her way out.*
FREDRIK *has now entered the bedroom,* ANNE *is no longer visible—as if she had moved into an inner room. In the parlor,* HENRIK *picks up the champagne bottle and glasses and puts them on the table*)

ANNE (*Off. Calling*) Fredrik!

FREDRIK Yes, dear.

38

ANNE (*Off*) Did you have many women between your first
wife and me? Sometimes when I think of what memories
you have, I vanish inside.

FREDRIK Before I met you I was quite a different man. Many
things were different. Better?

(ANNE *comes back into the bedroom*)

Worse? Different, anyway.

ANNE Do you remember when I was a little girl and you
came to my father's house for dinner and told me fairy
tales? Do you remember?

FREDRIK Yes, I remember.

ANNE (*Sitting on* FREDRIK'S *lap*) Then you were "Uncle
Fredrik" and now you're my husband. Isn't that amusing?
You were so lonely and sad that summer. I felt terribly
sorry for you, so I said: Poor thing, I'll marry him. Are you
coming to bed yet?

FREDRIK Not just yet. I think I'll go out for a breath of fresh
air.

ANNE That wasn't an amusing play, was it?

FREDRIK We didn't see that much of it.

ANNE I wonder how old that Armfeldt woman can be. At
least fifty—don't you think?

ⅇ

FREDRIK   I wouldn't say that old.

ANNE   Well, goodnight.

FREDRIK   Goodnight.

> (*As* FREDRIK *moves into the parlor,* MR. LINDQUIST *and* MRS. NORDSTROM *appear. There is a musical sting and* FREDRIK [*and* HENRIK] freeze)

MRS. NORDSTROM (*Sings*)
Remember?

MR. LINDQUIST (*Sings*)
Remember?

BOTH
Remember?
Remember?

> (FREDRIK unfreezes, *clasps his hands together and goes into the parlor.* HENRIK *looks anxiously at his* FATHER)

HENRIK   Is she all right now?

FREDRIK   Oh yes, she's all right.

HENRIK   It wasn't anything serious?

FREDRIK   No, nothing serious.

HENRIK   You don't think—a doctor? I mean, it would be terrible if it was something—serious.

FREDRIK   Pray for her, son. Correction—pray for me. Good-night.

HENRIK   Goodnight, father.

> (FREDRIK *exits, and* MRS. NORDSTROM *and* MR. LIND-QUIST *sweep downstage*)

MRS. NORDSTROM (*Sings*)
The local village dance on the green—
Remember?

MR. LINDQUIST (*Sings*)
Remember?
The lady with the large tambourine—
Remember?

MRS. NORDSTROM
Remember?
The one who played the harp in her boa
Thought she was so a-
Dept.

BOTH
Ah, how we laughed,
Ah, how we wept.
Ah, how we polka'd

MRS. NORDSTROM
And ah, how we slept.
How we kissed and how we clung—
Remember, darling?

A LITTLE NIGHT MUSIC

MR. LINDQUIST
We were foolish, we were young—

BOTH
More than we knew.

MRS. NORDSTROM
Yellow gingham on the bed,
Remember, darling?
And the canopy in red,

MR. LINDQUIST
Or was it blue?

> (MRS. NORDSTROM *and* MR. LINDQUIST *are joined by*
> MRS. SEGSTROM, MRS. ANDERSSEN *and* MR. ERLANSEN,
> *who appear downstage*)

MRS. SEGSTROM
The funny little games that we played—
Remember?

MR. ERLANSEN
Remember?
The unexpected knock of the maid—
Remember?

MRS. ANDERSSEN
Remember?
The wine that made us both rather merry
And, oh, so very
Frank.

42

ALL
> Ah, how we laughed.
> Ah, how we drank.

MR. ERLANSEN
> You acquiesced

MRS. ANDERSSEN
> And the rest is a blank.

MR. LINDQUIST
> What we did with your perfume—

MR. ERLANSEN
> Remember, darling?

MRS. SEGSTROM
> The condition of the room
> When we were through . . .

MRS. NORDSTROM
> Our inventions were unique—
> Remember, darling?

MR. LINDQUIST
> I was limping for a week,
> You caught the flu . . .

ALL
> I'm *sure* it was—
> You.

(They drift off as DESIREE'S *digs come on)*

DESIREE'S DIGS

FREDRIK *walks on, as* DESIREE, *in a robe, enters, munching a sandwich and carrying a glass of beer.*

FREDRIK They told me where to find you at the theater.

DESIREE Fredrik!

FREDRIK Hello, Desiree.

(*For a moment they gaze at each other*)

DESIREE So it *was* you! I peered and peered and said: "Is it . . . ? Can it be . . . ? Is it possible?" And then, of course, when you walked out after five minutes, I was sure.

FREDRIK Was my record that bad?

DESIREE Terrible. You walked out on my Hedda in Helsingborg. And on my sensational Phaedra in Ekilstuna.

44

FREDRIK (*Standing, looking at her*)   Fourteen years!

DESIREE   Fourteen years!

FREDRIK   No rancor?

DESIREE   Rancor? For a while, a little. But now—no rancor, not a trace.

(*Indicating a plate of sandwiches*)

Sandwich?

FREDRIK (*Declining*)   Hungry as ever after a performance, I see.

DESIREE   Worse. I'm a wolf. Sit down.

(*Pouring him a glass of schnapps*)

Here. You never said no to schnapps.

(FREDRIK *sits down on the love seat. She stands, looking at him*)

FREDRIK   About *this* walking out! I'd like to explain.

DESIREE   The girl in the pink dress, I imagine.

FREDRIK   You still don't miss a thing, do you?

DESIREE   Your wife.

FREDRIK   For the past eleven months. She was so looking forward to the play, she got a little overexcited. She's only eighteen, still almost a child.

(*A pause*)

I'm waiting.

DESIREE   For what?

FREDRIK   For you to tell me what an old fool I've become to have fallen under the spell of youth, beginnings, the blank page.

(*Very coolly,* DESIREE *opens the robe, revealing her naked body to him*)

DESIREE   The page that has been written on—*and* rewritten.

FREDRIK (*Looking, admiring*)   With great style. Some things —schnapps, for example—improve with age.

DESIREE   Let us hope that proves true of your little bride.

(*She closes the wrapper and stands, still very cool, looking at him*)

So you took her home and tucked her up in her cot with her rattle and her woolly penguin.

FREDRIK   Figuratively speaking.

DESIREE   And then you came to me.

FREDRIK   I wish you'd ask me why.

DESIREE (*Dead pan*)   Why did you come to me?

FREDRIK   For old times' sake? For curiosity? To boast about
my wife? To complain about her? Perhaps—Hell, why am
I being such a lawyer about it?

(*Pause*)

This afternoon when I was taking my nap . . .

DESIREE   So you take afternoon naps now!

FREDRIK   Hush! . . . I had the most delightful dream.

DESIREE   About . . . ?

FREDRIK   . . . you.

DESIREE   Ah! What did we do?

FREDRIK   Well, as a matter of fact, we were in that little hotel
in Malmo. We'd been basking in the sun all day.

DESIREE (*Suddenly picking it up*)   When my back got so
burned it was an agony to lie down so you . . . ?

FREDRIK   As vivid as . . . Well, *very* vivid! So you see. My
motives for coming here are what might be called—mixed.

(DESIREE *suddenly bursts into laughter*)

FREDRIK (*Tentative*)   Funny?

DESIREE (*Suddenly controlling the laughter, very mock solemn*) No. Not at all.

(*There is a pause, distinctly charged with unadmitted sex*)

FREDRIK (*Looking around, slightly uncomfortable*) How familiar all this is.

DESIREE Oh yes, nothing's changed. Uppsala one week. Orebroe the next. The some old inevitable routine.

FREDRIK But it still has its compensations?

DESIREE Yes—no—no—yes.

FREDRIK That's a rather ambiguous answer.

(*Pause*)

You must, at least at times, be lonely.

DESIREE (*Smiling*) Dear Fredrik, if you're inquiring about my love life, rest assured. It's quite satisfactory.

FREDRIK I see. And—if I may ask—at the moment?

DESIREE A dragoon. A very handsome, very married dragoon with, I'm afraid, the vanity of a peacock, the brain of a pea, but the physical proportions . . .

48

FREDRIK   Don't specify the vegetable, please. I am easily deflated.

(*They both burst into spontaneous laughter*)

Oh, Desiree!

DESIREE   Fredrik!

(*Another charged pause.* FREDRIK *tries again*)

FREDRIK   Desiree, I . . .

DESIREE   Yes, dear?

FREDRIK   I—er . . . That is . . .

(*Loses his nerve again*)

Perhaps a little more schnapps?

DESIREE   Help yourself.

(FREDRIK *crosses to the writing desk, where, next to the
schnapps, is a framed photograph of* FREDRIKA. *He no-
tices it*)

FREDRIK   Who's this?

DESIREE (*Suddenly rather awkward*)   That? Oh—my daughter.

FREDRIK   Your daughter? I had no idea . . .

✍

DESIREE She happened.

FREDRIK She's charming. Where is she now?

DESIREE She's with my mother in the country. She used to tour with me, and then one day Mother swept up like the Wrath of God and saved her from me—You never knew my mother! She always wins *our* battles.

(*Wanting to get off the subject*)

I think perhaps a little schnapps for me too.

FREDRIK Oh yes, of course.

(FREDRIK *pours a second schnapps. The charged pause again*)

DESIREE (*Indicating the room*) I apologize for all this squalor!

FREDRIK On the contrary, I have always associated you— very happily—with chaos.

(*Pause*)

So.

DESIREE So.

FREDRIK (*Artificially bright*) Well, I think it's time to talk about my wife, don't you?

DESIREE   Boast or complain?

FREDRIK   Both, I expect.

(*Singing*)

She lightens my sadness,
She livens my days,
She bursts with a kind of madness
My well-ordered ways.
My happiest mistake,
The ache of my life:
You must meet my wife.

She bubbles with pleasure,
She glows with surprise,
Disrupts my accustomed leisure
And ruffles my ties.
I don't know even now
Quite how it began.
You must meet my wife, my Anne.

One thousand whims to which I give in,
Since her smallest tear turns me ashen.
I never dreamed that I could live in
So completely demented,
Contented
A fashion.

So sunlike, so winning,
So unlike a wife.
I do think that I'm beginning
To show signs of life.
Don't ask me how at my age
One still can grow—
If you met my wife,
You'd know.

DESIREE   Dear Fredrik, I'm just longing to meet her. Some-
time.

FREDRIK (*Singing*)
She sparkles.

DESIREE (*Singing*)
How pleasant.

FREDRIK
She twinkles.

DESIREE
How nice.

FREDRIK
Her youth is a sort of present—

DESIREE
Whatever the price.

FREDRIK
The incandescent—what?—the—

DESIREE (*Proffering a cigarette*)

Light?

FREDRIK
—of my life!
You must meet my wife.

DESIREE
Yes, I must, I really must. Now—

FREDRIK
She flutters.

DESIREE
How charming.

FREDRIK
She twitters.

DESIREE
My word!

FREDRIK
She floats.

DESIREE
Isn't that alarming?
What is she, a bird?

FREDRIK
She makes me feel I'm—what?—

DESIREE
A very old man?

FREDRIK
Yes—no!

DESIREE
No.

A LITTLE NIGHT MUSIC

FREDRIK
But—

DESIREE
I must meet your Gertrude.

FREDRIK
My Anne.

DESIREE
Sorry—Anne.

FREDRIK
She loves my voice, my walk, my mustache,
The cigar, in fact, that I'm smoking.
She'll watch me puff until it's just ash,
Then she'll save the cigar butt.

DESIREE
Bizarre, but
You're joking.

FREDRIK
She dotes on—

DESIREE
Your dimple.

FREDRIK
My snoring.

DESIREE
How dear.

FREDRIK
The point is, she's really simple.

DESIREE (*Smiling*)
Yes, that much seems clear.

FREDRIK
She gives me funny names.

DESIREE
Like—?

FREDRIK
"Old dry-as-dust."

DESIREE
Wouldn't she just?

FREDRIK
You must meet my wife.

DESIREE
If I must—

(*Looks over her shoulder at him and smiles*)

Yes, I must.

FREDRIK
A sea of whims that I submerge in,
Yet so lovable in repentance.
Unfortunately, still a virgin,
But you can't force a flower—

DESIREE (*Rises*)
> Don't finish that sentence!
> She's monstrous!

FREDRIK
> She's frightened.

DESIREE
> Unfeeling!

FREDRIK
> Unversed.
> She'd strike you as unenlightened.

DESIREE
> No, I'd strike her first.

FREDRIK
> Her reticence, her apprehension—

DESIREE
> Her crust!

FREDRIK
> No!

DESIREE
> Yes!

FREDRIK
> No!

56

DESIREE
Fredrik . . .

FREDRIK
You must meet my wife.

DESIREE
Let me get my hat and my knife.

FREDRIK
What was that?

DESIREE
I must meet your wife.

FREDRIK   DESIREE
Yes, you must.   Yes, I must.

DESIREE (*Speaks*)   A virgin.

FREDRIK   A virgin.

DESIREE   Eleven months?

FREDRIK   Eleven months.

DESIREE   No wonder you dreamed of me!

FREDRIK   At least it was you I dreamed of, which indicates a
kind of retroactive fidelity, doesn't it?

A LITTLE NIGHT MUSIC

DESIREE   At least.

FREDRIK (*Suddenly very shy*)   Desiree, I—

DESIREE   Yes?

FREDRIK   Would it seem insensitive if I were to ask you—I can't say it!

DESIREE   Say it, darling.

FREDRIK   Would you . . .

(*He can't*)

DESIREE   Of course. What are old friends for?

(*She rises, holds out her hand to him.
He takes her hand, rises, too*)

Wait till you see the bedroom! Stockings all over the place, a rather rusty hip-bath—and the Virgin Mary over the headboard.

(*They exit, laughing, into the bedroom.
MADAME ARMFELDT appears and sings with one eye on the room*)

MADAME ARMFELDT
At the villa of the Baron de Signac,
Where I spent a somewhat infamous year,
At the villa of the Baron de Signac

I had ladies in attendance,
Fire-opal pendants . . .

Liaisons! What's happened to them?
Liaisons today.
Disgraceful! What's become of them?
Some of them
Hardly pay their shoddy way.

What once was a rare champagne
Is now just an amiable hock,
What once was a villa at least
Is "digs."

What was once a gown with train
Is now just a simple little frock,
What once was a sumptuous feast
Is figs.
No, not even figs—raisins.
Ah, liaisons!

Now let me see . . . Where was I? Oh yes . . .

At the palace of the Duke of Ferrara,
Who was prematurely deaf but a dear,
At the palace of the Duke of Ferrara
I acquired some position
Plus a tiny Titian . . .

Liaisons! What's happened to them?
Liaisons today.
To see them—indiscriminate
Women, it

A LITTLE NIGHT MUSIC

Pains me more than I can say,
The lack of taste that they display.

Where is style?
Where is skill?
Where is forethought?
Where's discretion of the heart,
Where's passion in the art,
Where's craft?
With a smile
And a will,
But with more thought,
I acquired a chateau
Extravagantly o-
Verstaffed.

Too many people muddle sex with mere desire,
And when emotion intervenes,
The nets descend.
It should on no account perplex, or worse, inspire.
It's but a pleasurable means
To a measurable end.
Why does no one comprehend?
Let us hope this lunacy is just a trend.

Now let me see . . . Where was I? Oh, yes . . .

In the castle of the King of the Belgians,
We would visit through a false chiffonier.
In the castle of the King of the Belgians

Who, when things got rather touchy,
Deeded me a duchy . . .

Liaisons! What's happened to them?
Liaisons today.
Untidy—take my daughter, I
Taught her, I
Tried my best to point the way.
I even named her Desiree.

In a world where the kings are employers,
Where the amateur prevails and delicacy fails to pay,
In a world where the princes are lawyers,
What can anyone expect except to recollect
Liai . . .

> (*She falls asleep.* FRID *appears and carries her off. A beat*)

CARL-MAGNUS (*Off-stage*) All right, all right. It's broken down. So *do* something! Crank it up—or whatever it is!

> (FREDRIK *and* DESIREE *appear at the bedroom door,* FREDRIK *in a bathrobe,* DESIREE *in a negligee*)

FREDRIK What can it be?

DESIREE It can't!

FREDRIK The dragoon?

DESIREE Impossible. He's on maneuvers. Eighty miles away.
He couldn't . . .

CARL-MAGNUS (*Off-stage, bellowing*) A garage, idiot! That's what they're called.

DESIREE He could.

FREDRIK Is he jealous?

DESIREE Tremendously.

(*Suppresses a giggle*)

This shouldn't be funny, should it?

FREDRIK Let him in.

DESIREE Fredrik . . .

FREDRIK I am not a lawyer—nor are you an actress—for nothing. Let him in.

(DESIREE *goes to open the door.* CARL-MAGNUS *enters, immaculate but brushing imaginary dust from his uniform. He is carrying a bunch of daisies*)

DESIREE (*With tremendous poise*) Carl-Magnus! What a delightful surprise!

(*Totally ignoring* FREDRIK, CARL-MAGNUS *bows stiffly and kisses her hand*)

The Opening Waltz. Act 1, Opening.

Victoria Mallory as Anne
Egerman. Act 1, Opening.

Van Williams

"Solitaire is the only thing in
life that demands absolute
honesty."
Madame Armfeldt (Her-
mione Gingold). Act 1, Pro-
logue.

"Don't they teach you anything at the seminary a little more cheerful?"
Henrik Egerman (Mark Lambert), Anne Egerman (Victoria Mallory).
Act 1, Scene 1.

Martha Swope

"Removing her clothing/Would take me all day."
Fredrik Egerman (Len Cariou). Act 1, Scene 1.

"We should make man's dignity our best ally and caress it . . ."
Mrs. Anderssen (Barbara Lang), Desiree Armfeldt (Glynis Johns), Mrs. Segstrom (Beth Fowler). Act 1, Scene 2.

"Hi-ho, the glamorous life!"
Desiree Armfeldt (Glynis
Johns). Act 1, Scene 1A.

Martha Swope

"Then you were 'Uncle Fredrik' and now you're my husband."
Anne Egerman (Victoria Mallory), Fredrik Egerman (Len Cariou). Act 1, Scene 3.

"I was limping for a week, You caught the flu . . ."
Mrs. Anderssen (Barbara Lang), Mr. Lindquist (Benjamin Rayson), Mrs. Nordstrom (Teri Ralston) Mrs. Segstrom (Beth Fowler), Mr. Erlansen (Gene Varrone). Act 1, Scene 3.

Martha Swope

Friedman-Abeles

"Too many people muddle sex with mere desire." Madame Armfeldt (Hermione Gingold). Act 1, Scene 4.

Martha Swope

"She wouldn't . . . / Therefore they didn't."
Count Carl-Magnus Malcolm (Laurence Guittard).
Act 1, Scene 4.

"I'll kill him.../ Why should I bother? / The woman's mine!"
Count Carl-Magnus Malcolm (Laurence Guittard),
Countess Charlotte Malcolm (Patricia Elliott). Act 1, Scene 5.

Van Williams

Martha Swope

CARL-MAGNUS Excuse my appearance. My new motorcar broke down.

(*Hand kiss. Presents the daisies*)

From a neighboring garden.

DESIREE (*Taking them*) How lovely! Will you be staying— long?

CARL-MAGNUS I have twenty hours leave. Three hours coming here, nine hours with you, five hours with my wife and three hours back.

(*Still ignoring* FREDRIK)

Do you mind if I take off my uniform and put on my robe?

DESIREE Well—at the moment it's occupied.

CARL-MAGNUS (*Not looking at* FREDRIK) So I see.

DESIREE Mr. Egerman—Count Malcolm.

FREDRIK Sir.

CARL-MAGNUS (*Still ignoring* FREDRIK) Sir.

FREDRIK   I feel I should give you an explanation for what may seem to be a rather unusual situation.

(*With tremulous aplomb*)

For many years, I have been Miss Armfeldt's mother's lawyer and devoted friend. A small lawsuit of hers—nothing major, I'm happy to say—comes up in Court tomorrow morning and at the last minute I realized that some legal papers required her daughter's signature. Although it was late and she had already retired . . .

DESIREE   I let him in, of course.

CARL-MAGNUS (*Turning the icy gaze on her*)   And then?

DESIREE   Ah, yes, the—the robe. Well, you see . . .

FREDRIK   Unfortunately, sir, on my way to the water-closet —through Miss Armfeldt's darkened bedroom—I inadvertently tripped over her hip-bath and fell in. Miss Armfeldt generously loaned me this garment while waiting for my clothes to dry in the bedroom.

CARL-MAGNUS   In that case, Miss Armfeldt, I suggest you return to the bedroom and see whether this gentleman's clothes are dry by now.

DESIREE   Yes. Of course.

(*She crosses between* FREDRIK *and* CARL-MAGNUS *and exits.*
   Pacing, CARL-MAGNUS *begins to whistle a military march.* FREDRIK *counters by whistling a bit of Mozart*)

CARL-MAGNUS   Are you fond of duels, sir?

FREDRIK   I don't really know. I haven't ever tried.

CARL-MAGNUS   I have duelled seven times. Pistol, rapier, foil. I've been wounded five times. Otherwise fortune has been kind to me.

FREDRIK   I must say I'm impressed.

CARL-MAGNUS (*Picking up fruit knife*)   You see this fruit knife? The target will be that picture. The old lady. Her face. Her eye.

   (*Throws knife, which hits target*)

FREDRIK (*Clapping*)   Bravo.

CARL-MAGNUS   Are you being insolent, sir?

FREDRIK   Of course—sir.

(DESIREE *returns from the bedroom. She is carrying* FREDRIK'S *clothes in a soaking wet bundle. She has dipped them in the hip-bath*)

65

DESIREE   They're not *very* dry.

FREDRIK   Oh dear me, they're certainly not, are they?

CARL-MAGNUS   A predicament.

FREDRIK   Indeed.

CARL-MAGNUS   I imagine, Miss Armfeldt, you could find this gentleman one of my nightshirts.

FREDRIK   Thank you, thank you. But I think I'd prefer to put on my own—er—garments.

(FREDRIK *takes the wet bundle from* DESIREE)

CARL-MAGNUS   Unfortunately, sir, you will not have the time for that.

(*To* DESIREE)

Perhaps you could tell him where to look.

DESIREE   Oh yes, yes. The left hand—no, the right hand bottom draw of the—er—

(*Indicating a chest of drawers*)

. . . thing.

(FREDRIK *gives her the wet clothes*)

FREDRIK (*Hesitating, then:*)   Thank you.

>(*He goes into the bedroom*
>   *While he is away,* DESIREE *and* CARL-MAGNUS *confront each other in near-silence:* CARL-MAGNUS *only whistles a bit of the march that he whistled at* FREDRIK *earlier*)

FREDRIK (*Returns in a nightshirt, carrying the robe, which he holds out to* CARL-MAGNUS)   Your robe, sir.

>(CARL-MAGNUS *receives it in silence.*
>   FREDRIK *puts on the nightcap that goes with the nightshirt*)

Well—er—goodnight. Miss Armfeldt, thank you for your cooperation.

>(FREDRIK *takes the wet bundle from* DESIREE *and exits*)

CARL-MAGNUS (*Singing, to himself*)
She wouldn't . . .
Therefore they didn't . . .
So then it wasn't . . .
Not unless it . . .
Would she?
She doesn't . . .
God knows she needn't . . .
Therefore it's not.

He'd never . . .
Therefore they haven't . . .
Which makes the question absolutely . . .
Could she?

A LITTLE NIGHT MUSIC

She daren't . . .
Therefore I mustn't . . .
What utter rot!

Fidelity is more than mere display,
It's what a man expects from life.

> (*The unit that* DESIREE *is sitting on starts to ride off
> as* CHARLOTTE, *seated at her breakfast table, rides on*)

Fidelity like mine to Desiree
And Charlotte, my devoted wife.

BREAKFAST ROOM IN MALCOLM COUNTRY
HOUSE

Breakfast for one (CHARLOTTE'S)—*and an extra coffee
cup—stands on an elegant little table. Music under.*

CHARLOTTE How was Miss Desiree Armfeldt? In good
health, I trust?

CARL-MAGNUS Charlotte, my dear. I have exactly five hours.

CHARLOTTE (*Dead pan*) Five hours this time? Last time it
was four. I'm gaining ground.

CARL-MAGNUS (*Preoccupied*) She had a visitor. A lawyer
in a nightshirt.

CHARLOTTE Now, *that* I find interesting. What did you do?

CARL-MAGNUS Threw him out.

CHARLOTTE   In a nightshirt?

CARL-MAGNUS   In *my* nightshirt.

CHARLOTTE   What sort of lawyer? Corporation, Maritime, Criminal—Testamentary?

CARL-MAGNUS   Didn't your sister's little school friend Anne Sorensen marry a Fredrik Egerman?

CHARLOTTE   Yes, she did.

CARL-MAGNUS   Fredrik Egerman.

(*He sings*)

The papers,
He mentioned papers,
Some legal papers
Which I didn't see there . . .
Where were they,
The goddamn papers
She had to sign?

What nonsense . . .
He brought her papers,
They were important
So he had to be there . . .
I'll kill him . . .
Why should I bother?
The woman's mine!

Besides, no matter what one might infer,
One must have faith to some degree.
The least that I can do is trust in her
The way that Charlotte trusts in me.
   (*Speaks*)

What are you planning to do today?

CHARLOTTE   *After* the five hours?

CARL-MAGNUS   Right now. I need a little sleep.

CHARLOTTE   Ah! I see. In that case, my plans will have to be changed. What will I do?

   (*Sudden mock radiance*)

I know! Nothing!

CARL-MAGNUS   Why don't you pay a visit to Marta's little school friend?

CHARLOTTE   Ah ha!

CARL-MAGNUS   She probably has no idea what *her* husband's up to.

CHARLOTTE   And I could enlighten her. Poor Carl-Magnus, are you *that* jealous?

CARL-MAGNUS   A civilized man can tolerate his wife's infidelity, but when it comes to his mistress, a man becomes a tiger.

71

CHARLOTTE   As opposed, of course, to a goat in a rut. Ah, well, if I'm back in two hours, that still leaves us three hours. Right?

CARL-MAGNUS (*Unexpectedly smiling*)   You're a good wife, Charlotte. The best.

CHARLOTTE   That's a comforting thought to take with me to town, dear. It just may keep me from cutting my throat on the tram.

(CHARLOTTE *exits*)

CARL-MAGNUS (*Sings*)
Capable, pliable . . .
Women, women . . .
Undemanding and reliable,
Knowing their place.
Insufferable, yes, but gentle,
Their weaknesses are incidental,
A functional but ornamental

(*Sips coffee*)

Race.
Durable, sensible . . .
Women, women . . .
Very nearly indispensable
Creatures of grace.
God knows the foolishness about them,
But if one had to live without them,
The world would surely be a poorer,
If purer, place.

The hip-bath . . .
About that hip-bath . . .
How can you slip and trip into a hip-bath?
The papers . . .
Where were the papers?
Of course, he might have taken back the papers . . .
She wouldn't . . .
Therefore they didn't . . .
The woman's mine!

   (*He strides off*)

THE EGERMAN ROOMS

In the bedroom, ANNE, *in a negligee, sits on the bed while* PETRA *combs her hair.*

ANNE   Oh, that's delicious. I could purr. Having your hair brushed is gloriously sensual, isn't it?

PETRA   I can think of more sensual things.

ANNE (*Giggles, then suddenly serious*)   Are you a virgin, Petra?

PETRA   God forbid.

ANNE (*Sudden impulse*)   I am.

PETRA   I know.

ANNE (*Astonished and flustered*)   How on earth can you tell?

74

PETRA   Your skin, something in your eyes.

ANNE   Can everyone see it?

PETRA   I wouldn't think so.

ANNE   Well, that's a relief.

   (*Giggles*)

How old were you when—

PETRA   Sixteen.

ANNE   It must have been terrifying, wasn't it? *And* disgusting.

PETRA   Disgusting? It was more fun than the rolly-coaster at the fair.

ANNE   Henrik says that almost everything that's fun is automatically vicious. It's so depressing.

PETRA   Oh him! Poor little puppy dog!

ANNE   (*Suddenly imperious*)   Don't you dare talk about your employer's son that way.

PETRA   Sorry, Ma'am.

ANNE   I forbid anyone in this house to tease Henrik.

(*Giggles again*)

Except me.

(ANNE *goes to the vanity, sits, opens the top of her robe, studies her reflection in the table-mirror*)

It's quite a good body, isn't it?

PETRA   Nothing wrong there.

ANNE   Is it as good as yours?

(*Laughing, she turns and pulls* PETRA *onto the bed, trying to undo* PETRA's *uniform*)

Let me see!

(*For a moment,* PETRA *is shocked. Laughing,* ANNE *continues,* PETRA *starts laughing too. They begin struggling playfully together*)

If I was a boy, would I prefer you or me? Tell me, tell me!

(*Still laughing and struggling they stumble across the room and collapse in a heap on the bed*)

You're a boy! You're a boy!

PETRA (*Laughing*)   God forbid!

(*As they struggle, the front doorbell rings*)

ANNE (*Sits up*)   Run, Petra, run. Answer it.

(PETRA *climbs over* ANNE *to get off of the bed.*
   As PETRA *hurries into the parlor and exits to answer the door,* ANNE *peers at herself in the mirror*)

Oh dear, oh dear, my hair! My—everything!

(PETRA *returns to the Parlor with* CHARLOTTE)

PETRA   Please have a seat, Countess. Madame will be with you in a minute.

(CHARLOTTE *looks around the room—particularly at* FREDRIK'S *picture—*
   PETRA *hurries in the bedroom. Hissing*)

It's a Countess!

ANNE   A Countess?

PETRA   Very grand.

ꕥ

ANNE   How thrilling! Who on earth can she be?

   (*After a final touch at the mirror, she draws herself up
   with great dignity and, with* PETRA *behind her, sweeps
   into the living room. At the door, she stops and stares.
   Then delighted, runs to* CHARLOTTE)

Charlotte Olafsson! It is, isn't it? Marta's big sister who
married that magnificent Count Something or other—and I
was a flower girl at the wedding.

CHARLOTTE   Unhappily without a time-bomb in your lilly of
   the valley bouquet.

ANNE   (*Laughing*)   Oh, Charlotte, you always did say the
   most amusing things.

CHARLOTTE   I still do. I frequently laugh myself to sleep contemplating my own future.

ANNE   Petra, ice, lemonade, cookies.

   (PETRA *leaves. Pause*)

CHARLOTTE   Well, dear, how are you? And how is your marriage working out?

ANNE   I'm in bliss. I have all the dresses in the world and a
   maid to take care of me and this charming house and a husband who spoils me shamelessly.

CHARLOTTE   That list, I trust, is in diminishing order of pri-
   ority.

78

ANNE   How dreadful you are! Of course it isn't. And how's dear Marta?

CHARLOTTE   Ecstatic. Dear Marta has renounced men and is teaching gymnastics in a school for retarded girls in Beetleheim. Which brings me or . . .

(Glancing at a little watch on her bosom)

. . . rather should bring me, as my time is strictly limited— to the subject of men. How do you rate your husband as a man?

ANNE   I—don't quite know what you mean.

CHARLOTTE   I will give you an example. As a man, my husband could be rated as a louse, a bastard, a conceited, puffed-up, adulterous egomaniac. He constantly makes me do the most degrading, the most humiliating things like . . . like . . .

(Her composure starts to crumble. She opens a little pocketbook and fumbles)

ANNE   Like?

CHARLOTTE   Like . . .

(Finding tiny handkerchief from purse, dabbing at her nose and bursting into tears)

Oh, why do I put up with it? Why do I let him treat me like—like an intimidated corporal in his regiment? Why? Why? Why? I'll tell you why. I despise him! I hate him! I *love* him! Oh damn that woman! May she rot forever in some infernal dressing room with lipstick of fire and scalding mascara! Let every billboard in hell eternally announce: Desiree Armfeldt in—in—in *The Wild Duck!*

(*Abandons herself to tears*)

ANNE   Desiree Armfeldt? But what has she done to you?

CHARLOTTE   What has she *not* done? Enslaved my husband —enslaved yours . . .

ANNE   Fredrik!

CHARLOTTE   He was there last night in her bedroom—in a nightshirt. My husband threw him out into the street and he's insanely jealous. He told me to come here and tell you . . . and I'm actually *telling* you! Oh what a monster I've become!

ANNE   Charlotte, is that the truth? Fredrik was there—in a nightshirt?

(CHARLOTTE *sobs*)

CHARLOTTE   My husband's nightshirt!

ANNE   Oh I knew it! I was sure he'd met her before. And when she *smiled* at us in the theater . . .

(*She begins to weep*)

80

CHARLOTTE   Poor Anne!

(PETRA *enters with the tray of lemonade and cookies
and stands gazing at the two women in astonishment*)

PETRA   The lemonade, Ma'am.

ANNE (*Looking up, controlling herself with a great effort, to
the weeping* CHARLOTTE)   Lemonade, Charlotte?

CHARLOTTE (*Looking up too, seeing the lemonade*)   Lemonade! It would choke me!

(*Sings*)

Every day a little death
In the parlor, in the bed,
In the curtains, in the silver,
In the buttons, in the bread.
Every day a little sting
In the heart and in the head.
Every move and every breath,
And you hardly feel a thing,
Brings a perfect little death.

He smiles sweetly, strokes my hair,
Says he misses me.
I would murder him right there
But first I die.
He talks softly of his wars,
And his horses
And his whores,
I think love's a dirty business!

81

A LITTLE NIGHT MUSIC

ANNE   So do I!

CHARLOTTE   ANNE
I'm before him   So do I . . .
On my knees
And he kisses me.

CHARLOTTE
  He assumes I'll lose my reason,
  And I do.
  Men are stupid, men are vain,
  Love's disgusting, love's insane,
  A humiliating business!

ANNE   Oh, how true!

CHARLOTTE   Ah, well . . .

ANNE
  Every day a little death,

CHARLOTTE
  Every day a little death,

ANNE
  On the lips and in the eyes,

CHARLOTTE
  In the parlor, in the bed,

CHARLOTTE   ANNE
In the curtains,   In the murmurs,
In the silver,   In the pauses,

CHARLOTTE
In the buttons,
In the bread.

ANNE
In the gestures,
In the sighs.

Every day a little dies,

Every day a little sting

In the looks and in
The lies.

In the heart
And in the head.

Every move and
Every breath,
And you hardly feel a
Thing,
Brings a perfect little
Death.

And you hardly feel a
Thing,
Brings a perfect little
Death.

(*After the number,* HENRIK *enters, taking off his hat
and scarf*)

HENRIK   Oh, excuse me.

ANNE (*Trying to rise to the occasion*)   Charlotte, this is Henrik Egerman.

HENRIK (*Bows and offers his hand*)   I am happy to make
your acquaintance, Madam.

83

CHARLOTTE   Happy! Who could ever be happy to meet *me*?

(*Holding* HENRIK'S *hand, she rises and then drifts out.* ANNE *falls back sobbing on the couch.* HENRIK *stands, gazing at her*)

HENRIK   Anne, what is it?

ANNE   Nothing.

HENRIK   But what did that woman say to you?

ANNE   Nothing, nothing at all.

HENRIK   That can't be true.

ANNE   It is! It is! She—she merely told me that Marta Olafs-son, my dearest friend from school is—teaching gymnas-tics . . .

(*Bursts into tears again, falls into* HENRIK'S *arms.* HENRIK *puts his arms around her slowly, cautiously*)

HENRIK   Anne! Poor Anne! If you knew how it destroys me to see you unhappy.

ANNE   I am not unhappy!

HENRIK   You know. You must know. Ever since you married Father, you've been more precious to me than . . .

ANNE (*Pulls back, suddenly giggling through her tears*) . . . Martin Luther?

(HENRIK, *cut to the quick, jumps up*)

HENRIK   Can you laugh at me even now?

ANNE (*Rises*)   Oh dear, I'm sorry. Perhaps, after all, I am a totally frivolous woman with ice for a heart. Am I, Henrik? *Am I?*

(PETRA *enters*)

MADAME ARMFELDT'S VOICE (*Off. Pushed in chair by* FRID) Seven of hearts on the eight of spades.

ANNE (*Laughing again*)   Silly Henrik, get your book, quick, and denounce the wickedness of the world to me for at least a half an hour.

(ANNE *runs off as the bedroom and parlor go.* HENRIK *follows her, as does* PETRA, *carrying the lemonade tray*)

MADAME ARMFELDT'S VOICE   The Ten of Hearts! Who needs the Ten of Hearts! !

ARMFELDT TERRACE

MADAME ARMFELDT *is playing solitaire with* FRID *standing behind her.* FREDRIKA *sits at the piano, playing scales.*

MADAME ARMFELDT   Child, I am about to give you your advice for the day.

FREDRIKA   Yes, Grandmother.

MADAME ARMFELDT   Never marry—or even dally with—a Scandinavian.

FREDRIKA   Why not, Grandmother?

MADAME ARMFELDT   They are all insane.

FREDRIKA   All of them?

MADAME ARMFELDT   Uh-hum. It's the latitude. A winter when the sun never rises, a summer when the sun never sets, are more than enough to addle the brain of any man. Further off, further off. You practically inhaled the Queen of Diamonds.

DESIREE (*Off*)   Who's home?

FREDRIKA (*Jumps up, thrilled*)   Mother!

(DESIREE *enters and* FREDRIKA *rushes to her, throwing herself into* DESIREE'S *arms*)

DESIREE   Darling, you've grown a mile; you're much prettier, you're irresistible! Hello, Mother.

MADAME ARMFELDT (*Continuing to play, unfriendly*)   And to what do I owe the honor of this visit?

DESIREE   I just thought I'd pop out and see you both. Is that so surprising?

MADAME ARMFELDT   Yes.

DESIREE   You're in one of your bitchy moods, I see.

87

A LITTLE NIGHT MUSIC

MADAME ARMFELDT   If you've come to take Fredrika back, the answer is no. I do not object to the immorality of your life, merely to its sloppiness. Since I have been tidy enough to have acquired a sizeable mansion with a fleet of servants, it is only common sense that my granddaughter should reap the advantages of it.

(*To* FREDRIKA)

Isn't that so, child?

FREDRIKA   I really don't know, Grandmother.

MADAME ARMFELDT   Oh yes you do, dear. Well, Desiree, there must be something you want or you wouldn't have "popped out." What is it?

DESIREE   All right. The tour's over for a while, and I was wondering if you'd invite some people here next weekend.

MADAME ARMFELDT   If they're actors, they'll have to sleep in the stables.

DESIREE   Not actors, Mother. Just a lawyer from town and his family—Fredrik Egerman.

MADAME ARMFELDT   In my day, one went to lawyers' offices but never consorted with their *families*.

DESIREE   Then it'll make a nice change dear, won't it?

MADAME ARMFELDT   I am deeply suspicious, but very well.

88

DESIREE (*Producing a piece of paper*)   Here's the address.

MADAME ARMFELDT (*Taking it*)   I shall send 'round a formal invitation by hand.

(*She snaps her fingers for* FRID. *As he wheels her off:*)

Needless to say, I shall be polite to your guests. However, they will not be served my best champagne. I am saving that for my funeral.

(FREDRIKA *runs to* DESIREE; *they embrace, and* freeze *in that pose. The screens divide the stage so that we see, in another area,* PETRA *bringing* ANNE *an invitation on a small silver tray*)

PETRA (*Sings*)
Look, ma'am,
An invitation.
Here, ma'am,
Delivered by hand.
And, ma'am,
I notice the station-
Ery's engraved and very grand.

ANNE
Petra, how too exciting!
Just when I need it!
Petra, such elegant writing,
So chic you hardly can read it.
What do you think?
Who can it be?
Even the ink—

🙢

No, here, let me . . .
"Your presence . . ."
Just think of it, Petra . . .
"Is kindly . . ."
It's at a chateau!
"Requested . . ."
Et cet'ra, et cet'ra,
". . . Madame Leonora Armf—"
Oh no!
A weekend in the country!

PETRA
We're invited?

ANNE
What a horrible plot!
A weekend in the country!

PETRA
I'm excited.

ANNE
No, you're not!

PETRA
A weekend in the country!
Just imagine!

ANNE
It's completely depraved.

PETRA
A weekend in the country!

ANNE
It's insulting!

PETRA
It's engraved.

ANNE
It's that woman,
It's that Armfeldt . . .

PETRA
Oh, the actress . . .

ANNE
No, the ghoul,
She may hope to
Make her charm felt,
But she's mad if she thinks
I would be such a fool
As to weekend in the country!

PETRA
How insulting!

ANNE
And I've nothing to wear!

91

ANNE and PETRA
A weekend in the country!

ANNE
Here!

(ANNE *gives the invitation back to* PETRA)

The last place I'm going is there!

(ANNE *and* PETRA *exit behind a screen.*
DESIREE *and* FREDRIKA unfreeze *and begin to move downstage*)

DESIREE (*Speaks*)   Well, dear, are you happy here?

FREDRIKA   Yes. I think so. But I miss us.

DESIREE   Oh, so do I!

(*Pause*)

Darling, how would you feel if we had a home of our very own with me only acting when I felt like it—and a man who would make you a spectacular father?

FREDRIKA   Oh I see. The lawyer! Mr. Egerman!

DESIREE   Dear child, you're uncanny.

(DESIREE *and* FREDRIKA freeze *once again, and the screens close in to provide a stagette for the appearance of* FREDRIK, ANNE, *and* PETRA)

92

PETRA (*Sings*)
Guess what, an invitation!

ANNE
Guess who, begins with an "A" . . .
Armfeldt—
Is that a relation
To the decrepit Desiree?

PETRA
Guess when we're asked to go, sir—
See, sir, the date there?
Guess where—a fancy chateau, sir!

ANNE
Guess, too, who's lying in wait there,
Setting her traps,
Fixing her face—

FREDRIK
Darling,
Perhaps a change of pace . . .

ANNE
Oh, no!

FREDRIK
A
Weekend in the country
Would be charming,
And the air would be fresh.

ANNE
A weekend
With that woman . . .

93

FREDRIK
In the country . . .

ANNE
In the flesh!

FREDRIK
I've some business
With her mother.

PETRA
See, it's business!

ANNE
. . . Oh, no doubt!
But the business
With her mother
Would be hardly the business I'd worry about.

FREDRIK and PETRA
Just a weekend in the country,

FREDRIK
Smelling jasmine . . .

ANNE
Watching little things grow.

FREDRIK and PETRA
A weekend in the country . . .

ANNE
Go!

FREDRIK
My darling,
We'll simply say no.

ANNE
Oh!

> (*They exit.*
>> FREDRIKA *and* DESIREE unfreeze)

FREDRIKA (*Speaks*) Oh Mother, I know it's none of my business, but . . . that dragoon you wrote me about—with the mustache?

DESIREE Oh, him! What I ever saw in him astounds me. He's a tin soldier—arms, legs, brain—tin, tin, tin!

> (*They* freeze *on the downstage bench.*
>> *The screens close in, providing a new playing area for* ANNE *and* CHARLOTTE)

ANNE (*Sings*)
A weekend!

CHARLOTTE
How very amusing.

ANNE
A weekend!

CHARLOTTE
But also inept.

A LITTLE NIGHT MUSIC

ANNE
A weekend!
Of course, we're refusing.

CHARLOTTE
Au contraire,
You must accept.

ANNE
Oh, no!

CHARLOTTE
A weekend in the country . . .

ANNE
But it's frightful!

CHARLOTTE
No, you don't understand.
A weekend in the country
Is delightful
If it's planned.
Wear your hair down
And a flower,
Don't use make-up,
Dress in white.
She'll grow older
By the hour
And be hopelessly shattered by
Saturday night.
Spend a weekend in the country.

ANNE
We'll accept it!

CHARLOTTE
I'd a feeling
You would.

BOTH
A weekend in the country!

ANNE
Yes, it's only polite that we should.

CHARLOTTE
Good.

> (ANNE *and* CHARLOTTE *both disappear behind the screens.*
> DESIREE *and* FREDRIKA *unfreeze*)

FREDRIKA Count Malcolm's insanely jealous, isn't he? You don't suppose he'll come galloping up on a black stallion, brandishing a sword?

DESIREE Oh dear, I hadn't thought of that. But no, no, thank heavens. It's his wife's birthday this weekend—sacred to domesticity. At least we're safe from him.

> (*They* freeze.
> CARL-MAGNUS *enters from behind a screen;* CHARLOTTE *follows opposite to meet him*)

A LITTLE NIGHT MUSIC

CARL-MAGNUS (*Sings*)
  Well?

CHARLOTTE
  I've an intriguing little social item.

CARL-MAGNUS
  What?

CHARLOTTE
  Out at the Armfeldt family manse.

CARL-MAGNUS
  Well, what?

CHARLOTTE
  Merely a weekend,
  Still I thought it might am-
  Use you to know who's invited to go,
  This time with his pants.

CARL-MAGNUS
  You don't mean—?

CHARLOTTE
  I'll give you three guesses.

CARL-MAGNUS
  She wouldn't!

CHARLOTTE
  Reduce it to two.

CARL-MAGNUS
It can't be . . .

CHARLOTTE
It nevertheless is . . .

CARL-MAGNUS
Egerman!

CHARLOTTE
Right! Score one for you.

CARL-MAGNUS (*Triumphantly*)
Aha!

CHARLOTTE (*Triumphantly*)
Aha!

CARL-MAGNUS (*Thoughtfully*)
Aha!

CHARLOTTE (*Worriedly*)
Aha?

CARL-MAGNUS
A weekend in the country . . .
We should try it—

CHARLOTTE
How I wish we'd been asked.

A LITTLE NIGHT MUSIC

ᴋ

CARL-MAGNUS
A weekend in the country . . .
Peace and quiet—

CHARLOTTE
We'll go masked.

CARL-MAGNUS
A weekend in the country . . .

CHARLOTTE
Uninvited—
They'll consider it odd.

CARL-MAGNUS
A weekend in the country—
I'm delighted!

CHARLOTTE
Oh, my God.

CARL-MAGNUS
And the shooting should be pleasant
If the weather's not too rough.
Happy Birthday,
It's your present.

CHARLOTTE
But . . .

CARL-MAGNUS
You haven't been getting out nearly enough,
And a weekend in the country . . .

CHARLOTTE
It's perverted!

CARL-MAGNUS
Pack my quiver and bow.

CHARLOTTE and CARL-MAGNUS
A weekend in the country—

CARL-MAGNUS
At exactly 2:30, we go.

CHARLOTTE
We can't.

CARL-MAGNUS
We shall.

CHARLOTTE
We shan't.

CARL-MAGNUS
I'm getting the car
And we're motoring down.

CHARLOTTE
Yes, I'm certain you are
And I'm staying in town.

(*The screens open to reveal* ANNE, FREDRIK, *and* PETRA)

CARL-MAGNUS   ANNE
Go and pack my suits!   We'll go.

101

A LITTLE NIGHT MUSIC

CHARLOTTE
I won't!

CARL-MAGNUS
My boots!
Pack everything I own
That shoots.

CHARLOTTE
No!

CARL-MAGNUS
Charlotte!

CHARLOTTE
I'm thinking it out.

CARL-MAGNUS
Charlotte!

CHARLOTTE
There's no need to shout.

CARL-MAGNUS
Charlotte!

CHARLOTTE
All right, then,

PETRA
Oh good!

FREDRIK
We will?

ANNE
We should.
Pack everything white.

PETRA
Ma'am, it's wonderful news!

FREDRIK
Are you sure it's all right?

ANNE
We'd be rude to refuse.

FREDRIK
Then we're off!

PETRA
We are?

FREDRIK
We'll take the car.

ALL THREE
We'll bring champagne
And caviar!
We're off on our way,
What a beautiful day
For

BOTH
We're off on our way,
What a beautiful day
For

ALL
   A weekend in the country,
   How amusing,
   How delightfully droll,
   A weekend in the country
   While we're losing our control.
   A weekend in the country,
   How enchanting
   On the manicured lawns.
   A weekend in the country,
   With the panting and the yawns.
   With the crickets and the pheasants
   And the orchards and the hay,
   With the servants and the peasants,
   We'll be laying our plans
   While we're playing croquet
   For a weekend in the country,
   So inactive that one has to lie down.
   A weekend in the country
   Where . . .

      (HENRIK *enters*)

HENRIK
   A weekend in the country,
   The bees in their hives,

The shallow worldly figures,
The frivolous lives.
The devil's companions
Know not whom they serve.
It might be instructive
To observe.

(DESIREE *and* FREDRIKA unfreeze)

DESIREE   However, there is one tiny snag.

FREDRIKA   A snag?

DESIREE   Lawyer Egerman is married.

FREDRIKA   That could be considered a snag.

DESIREE   Don't worry, my darling. I was not raised by your
Grandmother for nothing.

(DESIREE *holds out her arm, and* FREDRIKA *runs to her.
Together, they walk upstage as the screens open, revealing, for the first time, the facade of the Armfeldt
Mansion.* FRID *stands at the door, and once* DESIREE
and FREDRIKA *have entered, he closes it behind them*)

CARL-MAGNUS	FREDRIK	HENRIK
Charlotte!	We're off!	A weekend in the Country,
CHARLOTTE	PETRA	The bees in their
I'm thinking it out.	We are?	Hives . . .

CARL-MAGNUS Charlotte!	FREDRIK and ANNE We'll take the car.	

| CHARLOTTE
There's no need
To shout. | FREDRIK, ANNE, *and*
PETRA
We'll bring
Champagne and
Caviar! | MRS. SEGSTROM
and
MRS. ANDERSSEN
We're off! We are?
We'll take the car. |

| MRS. NORDSTROM
and MR. ERLANSEN
A weekend of
        playing
Croquet, | MR. LINDQUIST
Confiding our
       motives
And hiding our
       yawns, | We'll
Bring
Champagne |

| MRS. NORDSTROM
and MR. ERLANSEN
A weekend of
       strolling
The lawns, | | MRS. SEGSTROM and
MRS. ANDERSSEN
And caviar! |

CARL-MAGNUS, CHARLOTTE, FREDRIK, ANNE, *and* PETRA We're off and away, What a beautiful day!	ALL THE QUINTET The weather is spectacular!

ALL
   With riotous laughter
   We quietly suffer
   The season in town,
   Which is reason enough for

A LITTLE NIGHT MUSIC

A weekend in the country,
How amusing,
How delightfully droll!
A weekend in the country,
While we're losing our control.
A weekend in the country,
How enchanting
On the manicured lawns.
A weekend in the country,
With the panting and the yawns.
With the crickets and the pheasants
And the orchards and the hay,
With the servants and the peasants
We'll be laying our plans
While we're playing croquet
For a weekend in the country,
So inactive
That one has to lie down.
A weekend in the country
Where
We're twice as upset as in,
Twice as upset as in,
Twice as upset as in,
Twice as upset as in . . .

(ALL, *simultaneously*)

CARL-MAGNUS	CHARLOTTE
Charlotte, we're going!	We're uninvited!
Charlotte, we're going!	We're uninvited!
Charlotte, we're going!	We're uninvited!
Charlotte, we're going!	We should stay in . . .

106

ANNE	FREDRIK	PETRA
A weekend!	Are you sure you want to go?	A weekend!
A weekend!	Are you sure you want to go?	A weekend!
A weekend!	Are you sure you want to go	A weekend!
A weekend!	Away and leave,	A weekend!
A weekend!	Go and leave	A weekend!
A weekend!		A weekend!
A weekend!		A weekend!
A weekend		A weekend
In		In

HENRIK	THE QUINTET
World's shallow people going,	Twice as upset as in
Shallow world's people going	Twice as upset as in
To	Twice as upset as in
	Twice as upset as in
	Twice as upset as in
	Twice as upset as in
	Twice as upset as in
	Twice as upset as in

ALL
  Town!

Curtain

ENTR'ACTE

After a musical Entr' Acte, THE QUINTET *enters.*

MRS. ANDERSSEN
    The sun sits low,
    Diffusing its usual glow.
    Five o'clock . . .
    Twilight . . .
    Vespers sound,
    And it's six o'clock . . .
    Twilight
    All around,

ALL
    But the sun sits low,
    As low as it's going to go.

MR. ERLANSEN
    Eight o'clock . . .

MR. LINDQUIST
    Twilight . . .

108

GIRLS
How enthralling!

MR. ERLANSEN
It's nine o'clock . . .

MR. LINDQUIST
Twilight . . .

GIRLS
Slowly crawling towards

MR. ERLANSEN
Ten o'clock . . .

MR. LINDQUIST
Twilight . . .

GIRLS
Crickets calling,

ALL
The vespers ring,
The nightingale's waiting to sing.
The rest of us wait on a string.
Perpetual sunset
Is rather an unset-
Tling thing.

(The show curtain rises on Scene 1)

THE ARMFELDT LAWN

FRID *is serving champagne to* DESIREE *and* MALLA.
FREDRIKA, *upstage, is playing croquet with the help of*
BERTRAND, MADAME ARMFELDT'S *page.* FRID *returns to*
MADAME ARMFELDT. OSA *passes with a tray of cookies,
and* FREDRIKA *takes one.* DESIREE *gets a mallet and be-
gins to play croquet.*

MADAME ARMFELDT   To lose a lover or even a husband or
two during the course of one's life can be vexing. But to lose
one's teeth is a catastrophe. Bear that in mind, child, as you
chomp so recklessly into that ginger snap.

FREDRIKA   Very Well, Grandmother.

110

"Every day a little death."
Countess Charlotte Malcolm (Patricia Elliott), Anne Egerman (Victoria Mallory). Act 1, Scene 6.

Left: "Count Malcolm's insanely jealous, isn't he?" Fredrika Armfeldt (Judy Kahan), Desiree Armfeldt (Glynis Johns). Act 1, Scene 7.

Right: "They're coming!" Desiree Armfeldt (Glynis Johns). Act 2, Scene 1.

Below: "A weekend in the country." Act 1, Scene 7 (Finale).

Van Williams

"Mother will be honored!—surprised, but honored."
Countess Charlotte Malcolm (Patricia Elliott),
Fredrika Armfeldt (Judy Kahan), Count Carl-
Magnus Malcolm (Laurence Guittard), Desiree
Armfeldt (Glynis Johns), Fredrik Egerman (Len
Cariou), Anne Egerman (Victoria Mallory).
Act 2, Scene 1.

Fredrik comes out from behind the statue, laughing.
Fredrik Egerman (Len Cariou). Act 2, Scene 3.

Martha Swope

Van Williams

"Keeping control / While falling apart."
Mrs. Segstrom (Beth Fowler), Mrs. Anderssen (Barbara Lang), Mrs.
Nordstrom (Teri Ralston). Act 2, Scene 4.

Martha Swope

Above: "To Life!" Act 2, Scene 4.

Martha Swope

"Send in the clowns."
Desiree Armfeldt (Glynis Johns). Act 2, Scene 6.

Left: "What in God's name are we laughing about?"
Desiree Armfeldt (Glynis Johns), Fredrik Egerman (Len Cariou). Act 2,
Scene 6.

"There are mouths to be kissed / Before mouths to be fed." Petra (D. Jamin-Bartlett). Act 2, Scene 7.

Martha Swope

"Any man who thinks he can lay a finger on *my* wife!"
Count Carl-Magnus Malcolm (Laurence Guittard), Desiree Armfeldt (Glynis Johns). Act 2, Scene 8.

Martha Swope

MADAME ARMFELDT (*Holding up her glass to* FRID) More champagne, Frid.

(FRID *gets a fresh bottle*)

One bottle the less of the Mumms '87 will not, I hope, diminish the hilarity at my wake.

(DESIREE *sits on the rise.* FRID *opens the bottle with a loud* POP!)

THE QUINTET
The sun won't set.
It's fruitless to hope or to fret.
It's dark as it's going to get.
The hands on the clock turn,
But don't sing a nocturne
Just yet.

(*Off, we hear a car-horn*)

DESIREE They're coming!

MADAME ARMFELDT Nonsense!

DESIREE But they are!

111

᪥

MADAME ARMFELDT   Impossible. No guest with the slightest grasp of what is seemly would arrive before five-fifteen on a Friday afternoon.

(*We hear the car-horn again, and this time it's louder*)

Good God, you're right!

DESIREE   Malla!

(DESIREE *runs up into the house, followed closely by* MALLA, *and* OSA. BERTRAND *exits with the croquet set*)

MADAME ARMFELDT   Frid! We cannot be caught squatting on the ground like Bohemians!

(FRID *scoops her up and carries her into the house.* FREDRIKA *follows.*
   THE QUINTET *runs on to collect the furniture and props left on stage:* MR. ERLANSEN *gets the champagne buckets,* MRS. NORDSTROM *the fur rug,* MRS. ANDERSSEN *the cookie stand,* MR. LINDQUIST *the wickets and croquet pole,* MRS. SEGSTROM MADAME'S *wicker stool. They freeze for a moment at the sound of the car-horn, and then all run off.*
   A beat later, CARL-MAGNUS' *sports car drives on.* CARL-MAGNUS *is driving;* CHARLOTTE *sits beside him.* CARL-MAGNUS *stops the car and gets out*)

CHARLOTTE (*Looking around*)   Happy birthday to me!

CARL-MAGNUS (*Inspecting a wheel*)   What was that?

112

CHARLOTTE   I merely said . . . oh, never mind.

CARL-MAGNUS   If that damn lawyer thinks he's going to get away with something—Haha!

CHARLOTTE   Haha! indeed, dear.

(CARL-MAGNUS *helps* CHARLOTTE *out of the car*)

CARL-MAGNUS   Watch him, Charlotte. Watch them both like a . . .

CHARLOTTE   Hawk, I know, dear. You're a tiger, I'm a hawk. We're our own zoo.

(*As she speaks, a touring car sweeps on from the opposite side. It is driven rather erratically by* FREDRIK *with* ANNE *beside him.* HENRIK *and* PETRA *are in the back seat with a pile of luggage. The car only just misses* CARL-MAGNUS' *car as it comes to a stop.*
Recognition comes. FREDRIK *gets out of his car*)

FREDRIK   Good day, sir. I was not aware that you were to be a fellow guest.

(FREDRIK *opens the car and helps* ANNE *out.*
HENRIK *helps* PETRA *out of the back seat*)

CARL-MAGNUS   Neither is Miss Armfeldt. I hope our arrival will in no way inconvenience you.

↙

FREDRIK   Not at all, not at all. I am happy to see that you have gotten through yet another week without any serious wounds.

CARL-MAGNUS   What's that? Wounds, sir?

FREDRIK   Rapier? Bow and arrow? Blow dart?

(*At this point,* ANNE *and* CHARLOTTE *see each other. They run together.*
   On the way, ANNE *drops her handkerchief*)

ANNE (*Hissing*)	CHARLOTTE (*Hissing*)
So you did come?	So you did come?
(*Pause*)	(*Pause*)
Talk later.	Talk later.

(HENRIK, *tremendously solicitous, holds out the hand-kerchief to* ANNE)

HENRIK   Your handkerchief, Anne.

ANNE (*Taking it, moving away*)   Thank you.

HENRIK   You must have dropped it.

(PETRA *taps* HENRIK *on the shoulder*)

PETRA   Your book, Master Henrik.

HENRIK (*Taking it*)   Thank you.

114

PETRA (*With soupy mock-solicitousness*) You must have dropped it.

> (PETRA *moves to get the luggage.*
>   FRID, *seeing and immediately appreciating* PETRA, *goes to her*)

FRID Here. Let me.

PETRA (*Handing him two suitcases*) Let you—*what?*

> (PETRA, *with one suitcase, enters the house, followed by* FRID, *who is carrying two.* HENRIK *is moodily drifting away as* DESIREE *emerges from the house. She is followed by* FREDRIKA, *and smiling dazzlingly for the* EGERMANS)

DESIREE Ah, here you all are . . .

> (CARL-MAGNUS *clears his throat noisily. The smile dies*)

Count Malcolm!

CARL-MAGNUS (*Bowing frigidly over her hand*) My wife and I were in the neighborhood to visit her cousin. Unhappily, on arrival, we discovered the chateau was quarantined for . . .

> (*Flicks his fingers at* CHARLOTTE)

CHARLOTTE Plague.

CARL-MAGNUS   Since I am due back to maneuvers by dawn, we venture to propose ourselves for the night.

DESIREE (*Concealing no little fluster*)   Well, yes. Indeed. Why not? Mother will be honored!—surprised, but honored.

(DESIREE *crosses to* CHARLOTTE, *and sweeps past her, barely touching her hand*)

Countess Malcolm, I presume?

CHARLOTTE (*As* DESIREE *sweeps past her*)   You do indeed, Miss Armfeldt.

DESIREE   And Mr. Egerman! How kind of you all to come. Mother will be overjoyed.

FREDRIK (*Bending over her hand*)   It is your mother who is kind in inviting us. Allow me to present my rather anti-social son, Henrik.

(*Points to the drifting away* HENRIK, *who turns to acknowledge her*)

And this is my wife.

(*He presents* ANNE)

DESIREE   How do you do?

ANNE (*Icy*)   How do you do?

116

DESIREE (*Indicating* FREDRIKA)   And this is *my* daughter.

(*Pause*)

You must all be exhausted after your journeys; my daughter will show you to your rooms. Mother likes dinner at nine.

(FREDRIKA leads *them into the house:* CHARLOTTE, *then* ANNE, *then* HENRIK, *then* OSA. FREDRIKA *then stays on the terrace.*

Simultaneously, both FREDRIK *and* CARL-MAGNUS *turn, both with the same idea: to get* DESIREE *alone*)

CARL-MAGNUS and FREDRIK   Where shall I put the car?

(*They exchange a hostile glare*)

DESIREE (*Even more flustered*)   Ah, the cars, the cars! Now let me see.

CARL-MAGNUS (*Hissing*)   I must speak to you at once!

DESIREE (*Hissing*)   Later.

(*Out loud*)

How about the stables? They're straight ahead.

FREDRIK (*Hissing*)   I must speak to you at once!

117

A LITTLE NIGHT MUSIC

DESIREE (*Hissing*) Later.

> (*Reassured,* CARL-MAGNUS *and* FREDRIK *return to their cars.*
> *Calling after him*)

You can't miss them, Mr. Egerman. Just look for the weather vane. A huge tin cockerel.

> (*Spinning to* FREDRIKA, *pulling her downstage*)

Disaster, darling!

FREDRIKA But what are you going to do? The way he glared at Mr. Egerman! He'll kill him!

DESIREE Let us keep calm.

> (FREDRIK *and* CARL-MAGNUS, *both with auto-cranks in hand, start back toward* DESIREE)

FREDRIKA (*Noticing*) They're coming back!

DESIREE (*Totally losing her calm*) Oh no! Oh God!

> (DESIREE *starts to run up to the house*)

FREDRIKA (*Calling after her*) But what should I say?

DESIREE Anything!

> (*She runs into the house, as* FREDRIK *and* CARL-MAGNUS, *gazing after* DESIREE *in astonishment, come up to* FREDRIKA)

FREDRIKA (*On the spot but gracious, seemingly composed*)
Mr. Egerman—Count Malcolm . . . Mother told me to
tell you that she suddenly . . .

(*She breaks*)

. . . oh dear, oh dear.

(*She scurries up into the house.*
*The two men react, then, ignoring each other, return
to their cars. They each crank their cars and get into
them.*
The screens close in as the cars back out off-stage.
MR. ERLANSEN *and* MRS. NORDSTROM *enter*)

MRS. NORDSTROM (*Sings*)
The sun sits low
And the vespers ring,

MR. ERLANSEN
And the shadows grow
And the crickets sing,
And it's . . .

MRS. NORDSTROM
Look! Is that the moon?

MR. ERLANSEN
Yes.
What a lovely afternoon!

MRS. NORDSTROM
Yes.

A LITTLE NIGHT MUSIC

MR. ERLANSEN
 The evening air
 Doesn't feel quite right

MRS. NORDSTROM
 In the not-quite glare
 Of the not-quite night,
 And it's . . .
 Wait! Is that a star?

MR. ERLANSEN
 No.
 Just the glow of a cigar.

MRS. NORDSTROM
 Oh.

   (*They exit*)

THE OTHER PART OF THE GARDEN

ANNE *leads* CHARLOTTE *on. Both women carry parasols.*

ANNE   . . . After I spoke to you, I thought: I will go! I won't! Then I thought: Why not? We'll go to that awful woman's house and I'll say to her: "How dare you try to steal my husband? At your age you should have acquired at least some moral sense." And then—then in the motorcar coming here, I thought: "Oh dear, I'll never have the courage and maybe it's all my fault." And oh, I want to go home.

(*Bursts into sobs*)

CHARLOTTE   Have no fears. Miss Armfeldt has met her match.

ANNE (*Astonished, even through tears*)   She has? Who?

121

CHARLOTTE Me. When I told my husband, he instantly became a tiger—his word, of course—and then, as if from heaven, a plan flashed into my mind.

(*Pause*)

Do you feel up to hearing my plan, dear?

(ANNE *gives a little nod*)

I shall make love to your husband.

ANNE (*Aghast*) You too?

CHARLOTTE Confident of my own charms, I shall throw myself into your husband's arms. He will succumb. Why not? Carl-Magnus, in a storm of jealousy, will beg my forgiveness and swear eternal fidelity. And as for Miss Desiree Armfeldt, she will be back peddling her dubious commodities elsewhere. At least, that is the plan.

ANNE (*Suddenly forgetful of her tears*) Oh how amusing. How extremely amusing. Poor old Fredrik. And it serves him right, too.

CHARLOTTE I am not sure I appreciate that remark, dear.

(FREDRIK *appears, walking toward them*)

FREDRIK Ah, here you are, ladies.

CHARLOTTE (*Sudden devastating smile at* FREDRIK) Oh, Mr. Egerman! If you'll pardon my saying so, that's a simply ravishing cravat.

FREDRIK (*Slightly bewildered*) It is?

CHARLOTTE (*Taking* FREDRIK'S *left arm;* ANNE *takes his right arm*) I can't remember when I have seen so seductive a cravat.

(*As* ANNE *suppresses giggles, they all walk off together. As* ANNE, CHARLOTTE, *and* FREDRIK *exit,* MR. LINDQUIST *and* MRS. SEGSTROM *appear*)

MR. LINDQUIST (*Sings*)
The atmosphere's becoming heady,
The ambiance thrilling,

MRS. SEGSTROM
The spirit unsteady,
The flesh far too willing.

MR. LINDQUIST
To be perpetually ready
Is far from fulfilling . . .

MRS. SEGSTROM
But wait—
The sun
Is dipping.

A LITTLE NIGHT MUSIC

🖎

MR. LINDQUIST
 Where?
 You're right.
 It's dropping.
 Look—!
 At last!
 It's slipping.

MRS. SEGSTROM
 Sorry,
 My mistake,
 It's stopping.

   (*They exit*)

ACT II
Scene 2A

THE OTHER PART OF THE GARDEN

FREDRIKA *enters.*

FREDRIKA   Oh, I do agree that life at times can seem complicated.

(HENRIK *enters behind her*)

HENRIK   Complicated! If only you knew! Oh, Miss . . .
Miss . . .

FREDRIKA   Armfeldt. I am not legitimate.

HENRIK   I see. Oh, Miss Armfeldt, all my life, I've made a fiasco of everything. If you knew how poor an opinion I have of myself! If you knew how many times I wish I had been one of the spermatazoa that never reached the womb.

(*He breaks from her*)

There, there! You see? I've done it again!

FREDRIKA   Mr. Egerman, I have toured with mother, you know. I'm broadminded.

HENRIK   You are? Then in that case, might I make a confession to you?

FREDRIKA   Of course.

HENRIK   I hate to burden you on so slight an acquaintance, but bottling it up inside of me is driving me insane.

(*Pause. With great effort*)

Oh, Miss Armfeldt, for the past eleven months, although I am preparing to enter the Ministry, I—

(*He can't get it out*)

FREDRIKA   What, Mr. Egerman?

HENRIK   I have been madly, hopelessly in love with my stepmother. Do you realize how many mortal sins that involves? Oh, damn everything to hell! I beg your pardon.

(They link arms and walk off.
MR. LINDQUIST, MRS. SEGSTROM, MR. ERLANSEN, MRS. ANDERSSEN *and* MRS. NORDSTROM *enter and sing)*

ALL
The light is pink
And the air is still
And the sun is slinking
Behind the hill.
And when finally it sets,
As finally it must,
When finally it lets
The moon and stars adjust,
When finally we greet the dark
And we're breathing amen,

MRS. ANDERSSEN
Surprise of surprises,
It instantly rises
Again.

(THE QUINTET *exits*)

ARMFELDT TERRACE

Both dressed for dinner, FREDRIK *and* CARL-MAGNUS *are discovered;* FREDRIK *downstage,* CARL-MAGNUS *pacing on the porch.* FREDRIK *has a cigar and a small liqueur glass;* CARL-MAGNUS *carries a champagne glass.*

FREDRIK (*Sings*)
  I should never have
    Gone to the theater.
  Then I'd never have come
    To the country.
  If I never had come
    To the country,
  Matters might have stayed
  As they were.

CARL-MAGNUS (*Nods*)   Sir . . .

FREDRIK (*Nods*)   Sir . . .

If she'd only been faded,
If she'd only been fat,
If she'd only been jaded
And bursting with chat,
If she'd only been perfectly awful,
It would have been wonderful.
If . . . if . . .
If she'd been all a-twitter
Or elusively cold,
If she'd only been bitter,
Or better,
Looked passably old,
If she'd been covered with glitter
Or even been covered with mold,
It would have been wonderful.

But the woman was perfection,
To my deepest dismay.
Well, not quite perfection,
I'm sorry to say.
If the woman were perfection,
She would go away,
And that would be wonderful.

Sir . . .

CARL-MAGNUS   Sir . . .

If she'd only looked flustered
Or admitted the worst,
If she only had blustered

Or simpered or cursed,
If she weren't so awfully perfect,
It would have been wonderful.
If . . .
If . . .
If she'd tried to be clever,
If she'd started to flinch,
If she'd cried or whatever
A woman would do in a pinch,
If I'd been certain she never
Again could be trusted an inch,
It would have been wonderful.

But the woman was perfection,
Not an action denied,
The kind of perfection
I cannot abide.
If the woman were perfection,
She'd have simply lied,
Which would have been wonderful.

FREDRIK
If she'd only been vicious . . .

CARL-MAGNUS
If she'd acted abused . . .

FREDRIK
Or a bit too delicious . . .

CARL-MAGNUS
Or been even slightly confused . . .

130

FREDRIK
If she had only been sulky . . .

CARL-MAGNUS
Or bristling . . .

FREDRIK
Or bulky . . .

CARL-MAGNUS
Or bruised . . .

BOTH
It would have been wonderful.

CARL-MAGNUS
If . . .

BOTH
If . . .

FREDRIK
If she'd only been willful . . .

CARL-MAGNUS
If she only had fled . . .

FREDRIK
Or a little less skillful . . .

CARL-MAGNUS
Insulted, insisting . . .

A LITTLE NIGHT MUSIC

FREDRIK
In bed . . .

CARL-MAGNUS
If she had only been fearful . . .

FREDRIK
Or married . . .

CARL-MAGNUS
Or tearful . . .

FREDRIK
Or dead . . .

BOTH
It would have been wonderful.
But the woman was perfection,
And the prospects are grim.
That lovely perfection
That nothing can dim.
Yes, the woman was perfection,
So I'm here with him . . .

CARL-MAGNUS   Sir . . .

FREDRIK   Sir . . .

BOTH
It would have been wonderful.

(FREDRIKA *enters from the house*)

FREDRIKA   Excuse me, Count Malcolm, but Mother says she would like a word with you in the green salon.

> (CARL-MAGNUS, *glaring triumphantly at* FREDRIK, *jumps up and strides into the house.* FREDRIKA *stands and grins shyly at* FREDRIK, *then follows* CARL-MAGNUS *into the house.*
>
> DESIREE *enters*)

DESIREE   Fredrik, you wanted a moment alone with me, I believe. Here it is.

FREDRIK (*Puzzled*)   But that child said . . .

DESIREE   Oh, that was just Fredrika's little stratagem.

FREDRIK   Fredrika? Your child is called Fredrika?

DESIREE   Yes.

FREDRIK   Ah!

DESIREE   Really Fredrik, what vanity. As if you were the only Fredrik in the world.

> (*Brisk*)

Now, what is it you want to tell me?

FREDRIK   As a matter of fact, I thought you should know that my wife has no inkling of the nightshirt episode. So we should be discreet.

🖎

DESIREE   Dear Fredrik, of course. I wouldn't dream of giving that enchanting child a moment's anxiety.

FREDRIK   Then you do see her charm?

DESIREE   How could anyone miss it? How lovely to see you, Fredrik.

FREDRIK   In spite of Count Malcolm's invasion? You're sure we're not complicating . . .

CARL-MAGNUS (*Off*)   Desiree!

FREDRIK   Oh God! Something tells me I should make myself scarce.

CARL-MAGNUS (*Off*)   Desiree!

FREDRIK   Later, perhaps?

DESIREE   Any time.

FREDRIK   In your room?

DESIREE   In my room.

>   (FREDRIK *looks around for a place to hide. He finds the statue, puts his glass on it, and hides behind it. He douses his cigar in another glass resting on the statue*)

CARL-MAGNUS (*Comes out of the house*)   Desiree!

DESIREE (*Calling, excessively sweet*)   Here, dear!

CARL-MAGNUS   That child said the green salon.

DESIREE   She did? How extraordinary.

CARL-MAGNUS   Where's that goddamn lawyer?

DESIREE (*Airy*)   Mr. Egerman? Oh, somewhere about, no doubt.

CARL-MAGNUS   What's he doing here anyway?

DESIREE   He's visiting my mother, of course. He told you. They're the most devoted old friends.

CARL-MAGNUS   That had better be the truth. If I catch him so much as touching you, I'll call him out—with rapiers!

(*Glares*)

Where is your bedroom? Readily accessible, I trust.

DESIREE (*Aghast*)   But, Carl-Magnus!

(FRID *enters from the house, crosses downstage*)

With your *wife* here . . . !

CARL-MAGNUS Charlotte is irrelevant. I shall visit your bedroom at the earliest opportunity tonight.

FRID Madame, Count Malcolm! Dinner is served.

(*As he moves past them to pick up* FREDRIK'S *glass, he sees* FREDRIK *behind the statue. Totally unaware of complications*)

Dinner is served, Mr. Egerman.

(FRID *exits up into the house*)

DESIREE (*Rising to it*) Ah, there you are, Mr. Egerman!

(FREDRIK *comes out from behind the statue, laughing*)

Gentlemen, shall we proceed?

(*Gives one arm to each as they start up into the house and freeze in place*)

THE DINING ROOM

As the dining room table and GUESTS *come on,* MRS.
NORDSTROM, MRS. SEGSTROM *and* MRS. ANDERSSEN *sing.*

MRS. NORDSTROM
Perpetual
    anticipation is
Good for the soul
But it's bad for the
        heart.
It's very good for
    practicing

Self-control.
It's very good for
Morals,

MRS. SEGSTROM
Perpetual antici-
Pation is good for

The
Soul, but it's bad
For the
Heart.

137

A LITTLE NIGHT MUSIC

MRS. NORDSTROM
But bad for morale.
It's very bad.
It can lead to

Going quite mad.
It's very good for

Reserve and

Learning to do

What one should.
It's very good.

Perpetual
Anticipation's
A delicate art,

Playing a role,

Aching to start,

Keeping control
While falling
Apart.

MRS. SEGSTROM
It's very good for
Practicing self-
Control. It's
Very good for
Morals but bad
For morale. It's

Too unnerving.

It's very good,

Though, to have
Things to contem-

Plate.

Perpetual
Anticipation's
A
Delicate art,

Aching to start,

Keeping control
While falling
Apart.

MRS. ANDERSSEN
Per-
Petual antici-
Pation is good
For
The soul, but
It's
Bad for the
Heart.
It's
Very good,
Though,
To learn to
Wait.

Perpetual
Anticipation's
A
Delicate art,

Keeping control
While falling
Apart.

MRS. NORDSTROM	MRS. SEGSTROM	MRS. ANDERSSEN
Perpetual Anticipation is Good for the soul But it's bad for the	Perpetual Anticipation is Good But it's bad for the	Perpetual Anticipation is Bad for the
Heart.	Heart.	Heart.

(*The dining room table has moved onstage with* MAD-AME ARMFELDT *already seated in place, facing the audience in solitary splendor. The table is elaborately dressed with fruit and floral pieces and expensive din-nerware. There are also two large candelabra, one at each end of the table. Parallel to the table and upstage of it, the line of* SERVANTS *has come on:* BERTRAND, OSA, PETRA, *and* FRID. OSA *and* PETRA *stand with trays as* FRID *and* BERTRAND *light the candelabra.*

Once the table is in place, FREDRIK *and* CARL-MAGNUS *move up to it with* DESIREE. FREDRIK *pulls out a chair for* DESIREE *and she sits.* FREDRIK *gets* ANNE *and seats her.* CHARLOTTE *enters,* CARL-MAGNUS *seats her on the extreme right end of the table. He then moves to the ex-treme left, and sits down next to* DESIREE. HENRIK *sits between* DESIREE *and* ANNE, FREDRIK *between* ANNE *and* CHARLOTTE. *The* GUESTS *all sit facing upstage.* FRID *and* BERTRAND *pour, and* MADAME ARMFELDT *raises her glass. The* OTHERS *follow her. When the glasses come down, there is a burst of laughter and noise from the* GUESTS.

139

↙

> FREDRIKA, *seated at the piano, "accompanies" the scene*)

DESIREE   . . . So you won the case after all, Mr. Egerman! How splendid!

FREDRIK   I was rather proud of myself.

DESIREE   And I'm sure you were tremendously proud of him too, Mrs. Egerman.

ANNE   I beg your pardon? Oh, I expect so, although I don't seem to remember much about it.

> (CHARLOTTE *extends her glass;* BERTRAND *fills it*)

FREDRIK   I try not to bore my wife with my dubious victories in the courtroom.

DESIREE   How wise you are. I remember when I was her age, anything less than a new dress, or a ball, or a thrilling piece of gossip bored me to tears.

FREDRIK   That is the charm of youth.

CHARLOTTE   Dearest Miss Armfeldt, do regale us with more fascinating reminiscences from your remote youth.

CARL-MAGNUS   Charlotte, that is an idiotic remark.

140

FREDRIK   A man's youth may be as remote as a dinosaur, Countess, but with a beautiful woman, youth merely accompanies her through the years.

CHARLOTTE   Oh, Mr. Egerman, that is too enchanting!

(*Leaning over her chair*)

Anne, dear, where on earth did you find this simply adorable husband?

ANNE (*Leans. In on the "plan," of course, giggling*)   I'm glad you approve of him.

CHARLOTTE (*To* HENRIK)   Your father

(HENRIK *leans*)

is irresistible.

(CARL-MAGNUS *leans*)

I shall monopolize him for the entire week-end.

(DESIREE *leans*.
   Then, to ANNE)

Will you lease him to me, dear?

ANNE (*Giggling*)   Freely. He's all yours.

(FREDRIK *looks at* ANNE, *then at* CHARLOTTE, *then leans*)

. . . unless, of course, our hostess has other plans for him.

DESIREE (*Smooth, getting out of her seat*)   I had thought of seducing him into rolling the croquet lawn tomorrow, but I'm sure he'd find the Countess less exhausting.

CHARLOTTE (*Rising*)   I wouldn't guarantee that!

(*Clapping her hand over her mouth*)

Oh, how could those wicked words have passed these lips!

CARL-MAGNUS (*Astonished. Rising*)   Charlotte!

CHARLOTTE   Oh, Carl-Magnus, dear, don't say you're bristling!

(*To* FREDRIK *who has also risen. From here the two of them move to the music in a stylized fashion.*)

My husband, Mr. Egerman, is a veritable porcupine. At the least provocation he is all spines—or is it quills? Beware. I am leading you down dangerous paths!

CARL-MAGNUS (*Frigid*)   I apologize for my wife, sir. She is not herself tonight.

FREDRIK (*Both amused and gracious*)   If she is this charming when she is *not* herself, sir, I would be fascinated to meet her when she *is.*

CHARLOTTE   Bravo, bravo! My champion!

(HENRIK *and* ANNE *get up from the table and join the stylized dance*)

May tomorrow find us thigh to thigh pushing the garden roller in tandem.

FREDRIK (*Turning it into a joke*)   That would depend on the width of the rollers.

(*To* DESIREE)

Miss Armfeldt, as a stranger in this house, may I ask if your roller . . .

CARL-MAGNUS (*Instantly picking this up*)   Stranger, sir? How can you call yourself a stranger in *this* house?

FREDRIK (*Momentarily bewildered*)   I beg your pardon?

CARL-MAGNUS (*Triumphantly sure he has found* FREDRIK *and* DESIREE *out, to* MADAME ARMFELDT)   I understand from your daughter, Madame, that Mr. Egerman is an old friend of yours and consequently a frequent visitor to this house.

MADAME ARMFELDT (*Vaguely aware of him, peering through a lorgnette*) Are you addressing me, sir? Whoever you may be.

CARL-MAGNUS I am, Madame.

MADAME ARMFELDT Then be so kind as to repeat yourself.

DESIREE (*Breaking in*) Mother, Count Malcolm—

MADAME ARMFELDT (*Overriding this, ignoring her, to* CARL-MAGNUS) Judging from the level of the conversation so far, young man, you can hardly expect me to have been paying attention.

(CARL-MAGNUS *is taken aback*)

CHARLOTTE Splendid! The thrust direct! I shall commandeer that remark and wreak havoc with it at all my husband's regimental dinner parties!

(DANCE SECTION.
Finally MADAME ARMFELDT *tings on a glass with her fork for silence*)

MADAME ARMFELDT (*As* FRID *and* BERTRAND *serve*) Ladies and gentlemen, tonight I am serving you a very special dessert wine. It is from the cellars of the King of the Belgians who—during a period of intense intimacy—presented me with all the bottles then in existence. The secret of its unique quality is unknown, but it is said to possess the power to open the eyes—even of the blindest among us . . .

(*Raising her glass*)

To Life!

(*The* GUESTS *all raise their glasses*)

THE OTHERS To Life!

MADAME ARMFELDT And to the only other reality—Death!

(*Only* MADAME ARMFELDT *and* CHARLOTTE *drink.*
A sudden chilly silence descends on the party as if a huge shadow had passed over it. The GUESTS *slowly drift back to the table in silence.*
At length the silence is broken by a little tipsy giggle from CHARLOTTE)

CHARLOTTE Oh I *am* enjoying myself! What an unusual sensation!

(*Raises her glass to* DESIREE)

Dearest Miss Armfeldt, at this awe-inspiring moment—let me drink to *you* who have made this evening possible. The One and Only Desiree Armfeldt, beloved of hundreds—regardless of course of their matrimonial obligations!

(*Hiccups*)

CARL-MAGNUS Charlotte, you will go to your room immediately.

(*There is general consternation*)

FREDRIK Miss Armfeldt, I'm sure the Countess—

ANNE Oh, dear, oh, dear, I am beside myself.

HENRIK (*Suddenly jumping up, shouting, smashing his glass on the table*) Stop it! All of you! Stop it!

(*There is instantly silence*)

FREDRIK Henrik!

HENRIK (*Swinging to glare at him*) Are *you* reproving *me*?

FREDRIK I think, if I were you, I would sit down.

HENRIK   Sit, Henrik. Stand, Henrik. Am I to spend the rest
of my life at your command, like a lapdog? Am I to respect
a man who can permit such filthy pigs' talk in front of the
purest, the most innocent, the most wonderful . . . ? I despise you all!

ANNE   (*Giggling nervously*)   Oh Henrik! How comical you
look!

DESIREE   (*Smiling, holding out her glass to him*)   Smash this
too. Smash every glass in the house if you feel like it.

HENRIK   (*Bewildered and indignant*)   And you! You're an
artist! You play Ibsen and—and Racine! Don't any of the
great truths of the artists, come through to you at all? Are
you no better than the others?

DESIREE   Why don't you just laugh at us all, my dear?
Wouldn't that be a solution?

HENRIK   How can I laugh, when life makes me want to
vomit?

(*He runs out of the room*)

ANNE   Poor silly Henrik. Someone should go after him.

(*She gets up from the table, starts away*)

FREDRIK (*Very authoritative*) Anne. Come back.

> (*Meekly,* ANNE *obeys, sitting down again at the table. Total silence.* FREDRIK *sits. Then, after a beat:*
> *A hiccup from* CHARLOTTE)

DESIREE Dear Countess, may I suggest that you try holding your breath—for a very long time?

> (*The screens close in on the scene, and the table moves off*)

ARMFELDT GARDEN

HENRIK, *who has run from the dining room, runs and stands near the bench in despair.* FREDRIKA, *at the piano sees him.*

FREDRIKA (*Stops playing*)   Mr. Egerman!

(HENRIK *ignores her*)

Mr. Egerman?

(HENRIK *looks up*)

HENRIK   I have disgraced myself—acting like a madman, breaking an expensive glass, humiliating myself in front of them all.

FREDRIKA   Poor, Mr. Egerman!

HENRIK (*Defending himself in spite of himself*)   They laughed at me. Even Anne. She said, "Silly Henrik, how comical you look!" Laughter! How I detest it! Your mother

149

—everyone—says, "Laugh at it all." If all you can do is laugh at the cynicism, the frivolity, the lack of heart—then I'd rather be dead.

ANNE (*Off*)   Henrik!

HENRIK   Oh God! There she is!

(*He runs off*)

ANNE (*Off*)   Henrik dear!

FREDRIKA (*Calls after him*)   Mr. Egerman! Please don't do anything rash!

(ANNE *runs on*)

Oh Mrs. Egerman, I'm so terribly worried.

ANNE   You poor dear. What about?

FREDRIKA   About Mr. Egerman—Junior, that is.

ANNE   Silly Henrik! I was just coming out to scold him.

FREDRIKA   I am so afraid he may do himself an injury.

ANNE   How delightful to be talking to someone younger than myself. No doubt he has been denouncing the wickedness of the world—and quoting Martin Luther? Dearest Fredrika, all you were witnessing was the latest crisis in his love affair with God.

FREDRIKA   Not with God, Mrs. Egerman—with you!

ANNE *(Totally surprised)*   Me!

FREDRIKA   You may not have noticed, but he is madly, hope-lessly in love with you.

ANNE   Is that really the truth?

FREDRIKA   Yes, he told me so himself.

ANNE *(Thrilled, flattered, perhaps more)*   The poor dear boy! How ridiculous of him—and yet how charming. Dear friend, if you knew how insecure I constantly feel, how complicated the marriage state seems to be. I adore old Fredrik, of course, but . . .

FREDRIKA *(Interrupting)*   But Mrs. Egerman, he ran down towards the lake!

ANNE *(Laughing)*   To gaze over the ornamental waters! How touching! Let us go and find him.

(ANNE *takes* FREDRIKA's *arm and starts walking off with her*)

Such a good looking boy, isn't he? Such long, long lashes . . .

(*They exit giggling, arm-in-arm*)

ANOTHER PART OF THE GARDEN

FRID *runs on from behind a screen, followed by a more leisurely* PETRA. *They have a bottle of wine and a small bundle of food with them.*

PETRA Who needs a haystack? Anything you've got to show, you can show me right here—that is, if you're in the mood.

FRID (*Taking her into his arms*) When am I not in the mood?

PETRA (*Laughing*) I wouldn't know, would I? I'm just passing through.

FRID I'm in the mood.

(*Kiss*)

I'm in it twenty-four hours a day.

(*Kiss.*
FREDRIKA *runs across stage*)

152

FREDRIKA Mr. Egerman!

PETRA Private here, isn't it?

>(ANNE *runs across stage*)

ANNE Henrik! Henrik!

PETRA What *are* they up to?

FRID Oh, them! What are they ever up to?

>(ANNE *runs back across*)

ANNE Henrik!

>(FREDRIKA *runs back across*)

FREDRIKA Mr. Egerman!

FRID You saw them all at dinner, dressed up like waxworks, jabbering away to prove how clever they are. And never knowing what they miss.

>(*Kiss*)

ANNE'S VOICE Henrik!

A LITTLE NIGHT MUSIC

🖎

FRID   Catch one of them having the sense to grab the first
pretty girl that comes along—and do her on the soft grass,
with the summer night just smiling down.

(*Kiss*)

Any complaints yet?

PETRA   Give me time.

FRID   You've a sweet mouth—sweet as honey.

(*The screen moves, wiping out* FRID *and* PETRA. *It re-
veals* HENRIK, *who has been watching them make love.
After an anguished moment, he runs straight up into the
house, slamming the doors behind him*)

DESIREE'S BEDROOM

> DESIREE *sits on the bed, her long skirt drawn up over*
> *her knees, expertly sewing up a hem.*
> FREDRIK *enters and clears his throat.*

FREDRIK   Your dragoon and his wife are glowering at each
other in the Green Salon, and all the children appear to
have vanished, so when I saw you sneaking up the stairs . . .

DESIREE   I ripped my hem on the dining room table in all
that furor.

FREDRIK (*Hovering*)   Is this all right?

DESIREE   Of course. Sit down.

> (*Patting the bed beside her, on which tumbled stock-*
> *ings are strewn*)

FREDRIK   *On* the stockings?

DESIREE   I don't see why not.

(*There is a long pause*)

Well, we're back at the point where we were so rudely interrupted last week, aren't we?

FREDRIK   Not quite. If you'll remember, we'd progressed a step further.

DESIREE   How true.

FREDRIK   I imagine neither of us is contemplating a repeat performance.

DESIREE   Good heavens, with your wife in the house, and my lover and his wife and my daughter . . .

FREDRIK   . . . and my devoted old friend, your mother.

(*They both laugh*)

DESIREE   (*During it, like a naughty girl*)   Isn't my dragoon awful?

FREDRIK   (*Laughs*)   When you told me he had the brain of a pea, I think you were being generous.

(*They laugh more uproariously*)

DESIREE   What in God's name are we laughing about? Your son was right at dinner. We don't fool that boy, not for a moment. The One and Only Desiree Armfeldt, dragging

around the country in shoddy tours, carrying on with someone else's dim-witted husband. And the Great Lawyer Egerman, busy renewing his unrenewable youth.

FREDRIK   Bravo! Probably that's an accurate description of
us both.

DESIREE   Shall I tell you why I really invited you here? When
we met again and we made love, I thought: Maybe here
it is at last—a chance to turn back, to find some sort of
coherent existence after so many years of muddle.

(*Pause*)

Of course, there's your wife. But I thought: perhaps—just
perhaps—you might be in need of rescue too.

FREDRIK   From renewing my unrenewable youth?

DESIREE (*Suddenly tentative*)   It was only a thought.

FREDRIK   When my eyes are open and I look at you, I see a
woman that I have loved for a long time, who entranced
me all over again when I came to her rooms . . . who
gives me such genuine pleasure that, in spite of myself,
I came here for the sheer delight of being with her again.
The woman who could rescue me? Of course.

(*Pause*)

But when my eyes are not open—which is most of the time
—all I see is a girl in a pink dress teasing a canary, running
through a sunlit garden to hug me at the gate, as if I'd

157

come home from Timbuctu instead of the Municipal Court-
house three blocks away . . .

DESIREE (*Sings*)
Isn't it rich?
Are we a pair?
Me here at last on the ground,
You in mid-air.
Send in the clowns.

Isn't it bliss?
Don't you approve?
One who keeps tearing around,
One who can't move.
Where are the clowns?
Send in the clowns.

Just when I'd stopped
Opening doors,
Finally knowing
The one that I wanted was yours,
Making my entrance again
With my usual flair,
Sure of my lines,
No one is there.

(FREDRIK *rises*)

Don't you love farce?
My fault, I fear.

I thought that you'd want what I want—
Sorry, my dear.
But where are the clowns?
Quick, send in the clowns.
Don't bother, they're here.

FREDRIK   Desiree, I'm sorry. I should never have come. To flirt with rescue when one has no intention of being saved . . . Do try to forgive me.

(*He exits*)

DESIREE
Isn't it rich?
Isn't it queer?
Losing my timing this late
In my career?
And where are the clowns?
There ought to be clowns.
Well, maybe next year . . .

(*The lights iris out on* DESIREE)

THE TREES

As DESIREE'S *bedroom goes off,* HENRIK *emerges from the house, carrying a rope. He runs downstage with it.*
    ANNE *and* FREDRIKA *run on; when* HENRIK *hears them, he runs behind the screens to hide.*

ANNE (*As she runs on*)   Henrik!

    (*To* FREDRIKA)

Oh, I'm quite puffed! Where can he be?

    (*Noticing* FREDRIKA'S *solemn face*)

Poor child, that face! Don't look so solemn. Where would you go if you were he?

FREDRIKA   Well, the summer pavilion? And then, of course, there's the stables.

ANNE   Then you go to the stables and I'll take the summer pavilion.

(*Laughing*)

Run!

(*She starts off*)

Isn't this exciting after that stodgy old dinner!

(*They run off, and* HENRIK *runs back on. He stops at the trees, stands on the marble bench, and, after circling his noose around his neck, throws the other end of the rope up to the tree limb*)

ANNE'S VOICE   Henrik!

(HENRIK *falls with a loud thud, as* ANNE *enters*)

ANNE   What an extraordinary . . . ! Oh, Henrik—how comical you look!

(*Pulling him up by the noose still around his neck*)

Oh, no! You didn't!

(*Pause*)

For me?

161

🖎

(*She gently removes the noose from his neck*)

Oh, my poor darling Henrik.

(*She throws herself into his arms*)

Oh, my poor boy! Oh, those eyes, gazing at me like a lost Saint Bernard . . .

(*They start to kiss passionately*)

HENRIK   I love you! I've actually *said* it!

ANNE (*Returning his kisses passionately*)   Oh how scatter-brained I was never to have realized. Not Fredrik . . . not poor old Fredrik . . . not Fredrik at all!

(*They drop down onto the ground and start to make passionate love.
       The trees wipe them out, revealing* PETRA *and* FRID. FRID *is still asleep*)

PETRA (*Sings*)
I shall marry the miller's son,
Pin my hat on a nice piece of property.
Friday nights, for a bit of fun,
We'll go dancing.
Meanwhile . . .
It's a wink and a wiggle
And a giggle in the grass
And I'll trip the light fanadango,
A pinch and a diddle

In the middle of what passes by.
It's a very short road
From the pinch and the punch
To the paunch and the pouch and the pension.
It's a very short road
To the ten thousandth lunch
And the belch and the grouch and the sigh.
In the meanwhile,
There are mouths to be kissed
Before mouths to be fed,
And a lot in between
In the meanwhile.
And a girl ought to celebrate what passes by.

Or I shall marry the businessman,
Five fat babies and lots of security.
Friday nights, if we think we can,
We'll go dancing.
Meanwhile . . .
It's a push and a fumble
And a tumble in the sheets
And I'll foot the highland fancy,
A dip in the butter
And a flutter with what meets my eye.
It's a very short fetch
From the push and the whoop
To the squint and the stoop and the mumble.
It's not much of a stretch
To the cribs and the croup
And the bosoms that droop and go dry.
In the meanwhile,

A LITTLE NIGHT MUSIC

There are mouths to be kissed
Before mouths to be fed,
And there's many a tryst
And there's many a bed
To be sampled and seen
In the meanwhile.
And a girl has to celebrate what passes by.

Or I shall marry the Prince of Wales—
Pearls and servants and dressing for festivals.
Friday nights, with him all in tails,
We'll have dancing.
Meanwhile . . .
It's a rip in the bustle
And a rustle in the hay
And I'll pitch the quick fantastic,
With flings of confetti
And my petticoats away up high.
It's a very short way
From the fling that's for fun
To the thigh pressing under the table.
It's a very short day
Till you're stuck with just one
Or it has to be done on the sly.
In the meanwhile,
There are mouths to be kissed
Before mouths to be fed,
And there's many a tryst
And there's many a bed.
There's a lot I'll have missed

But I'll not have been dead when I die!
And a person should celebrate everything
Passing by.

And I shall marry the miller's son.

(*She smiles, as the lights fade on her*)

ACT II
Scene 8

ARMFELDT HOUSE AND GARDEN

FREDRIKA *is lying on the grass reading.* MADAME ARM-FELDT, *seated in a huge wingchair upstage.* DESIREE, *on the bed, is writing in her diary.* CARL-MAGNUS *paces on the terrace and then goes into the house.* MRS. SEG-STROM *and* MR. LINDQUIST *are behind trees,* MR. ERLAN-SEN *and* MRS. ANDERSSEN *are behind opposite trees. Charlotte sits downstage on a bench.*

After a beat, FREDRIK *enters, sees the* FIGURE *on the bench. Is it* ANNE? *He hurries toward her.*

FREDRIK   Anne?—Oh, forgive me, Countess. I was looking for my wife.

CHARLOTTE (*Looking up, through sobs*)   Oh Mr. Egerman, how can I face you after that exhibition at dinner? Throwing myself at your head!

FREDRIK   On the contrary, I found it most morale-building.

(*Sits down next to her*)

It's not often these days that a beautiful woman does me that honor.

CHARLOTTE   I didn't.

FREDRIK   I beg your pardon?

CHARLOTTE   I didn't do you that honor. It was just a charade. A *failed* charade! In my madness I thought I could make my husband jealous.

FREDRIK   I'm afraid marriage isn't one of the easier relation- ships, is it?

CHARLOTTE   Mr. Egerman, for a woman it's impossible!

FREDRIK   It's not all that possible for men.

CHARLOTTE   Men! Look at you—a man of an age when a woman is lucky if a drunken alderman pinches her derierre at a village fete! And yet, you have managed to acquire the youngest, prettiest . . . I hate you being happy. I hate *any- one* being happy!

(HENRIK *and* ANNE *emerge from the house, carrying suit- cases. They start stealthily downstage*)

A LITTLE NIGHT MUSIC

HENRIK   The gig should be ready at the stables.

ANNE (*Giggling*)   Oh Henrik darling, I do hope the horses will be smart. I do detest riding in a gig when the horses are not smart.

(HENRIK *stops, pulls her to him. They kiss*)

MRS. SEGSTROM (*Turns, looking onstage, sings*)
Think of how I adore you,
Think of how much you love me,
If I were perfect for you,
Wouldn't you tire of me
Soon . . . ?

HENRIK   Let all the birds nest in my hair!

ANNE   Silly Henrik! Quick, or we'll miss the train!

(THEY *are now downstage. Unaware of* FREDRIK *and* CHARLOTTE, *they move past them. For a long moment,* FREDRIK *and* CHARLOTTE *sit, while* FREDRIK'S *world tumbles around his ears*)

CHARLOTTE   It was, wasn't it?

FREDRIK   It was.

CHARLOTTE   Run after them. Quick. You can catch them at the stables.

FREDRIK (*Even more quiet*)   After the horse has gone?

(*Pause*)

How strange that one's life should end sitting on a bench in a garden.

MR. ERLANSEN (*Leans, looking onstage, sings*)
She lightens my sadness,
She livens my days,
She bursts with a kind of madness
My well-ordered ways.
My happiest mistake,
The ache of my life . . .

(*As they sit, the lights come up on* DESIREE'S BEDROOM, *as* CARL-MAGNUS *enters*)

DESIREE   Carl-Magnus, go away!

CARL-MAGNUS (*Ignoring her, beginning to unbutton his tunic*)
I'd have been here half an hour ago if I hadn't had to knock a little sense into my wife.

DESIREE   Carl-Magnus, do not take off your tunic!

CARL-MAGNUS (*Still ignoring her*)   Poor girl. She was somewhat the worse for wine, of course. Trying to make me believe that she was attracted to that asinine lawyer fellow.

DESIREE   Carl-Magnus, listen to me! It's over. It was never anything in the first place, but now it's OVER!

A LITTLE NIGHT MUSIC

CARL-MAGNUS (*Ignoring this, totally self-absorbed*)   Of all people—that lawyer! Scrawny as a scarecrow and without a hair on his body, probably.

(*He starts removing his braces*)

DESIREE (*Shouting*)   Don't take off your trousers!

CARL-MAGNUS (*Getting out of his trousers*)   Poor girl, she'd slash her wrists before she'd let any other man touch her. And even if, under the influence of wine, she did stray a bit, how ridiculous to imagine I would so much as turn a hair!

(*As he starts to get out of his trouser leg, he stumbles so that he happens to be facing the "window." He stops dead, peering out*)

Good God!

DESIREE   What is it?

CARL-MAGNUS (*Peering*)   It's her! And him! Sitting on a bench! She's touching him! The scoundrel! The conniving swine! Any man who thinks he can lay a finger on *my* wife!

(*Pulling up his pants and grabbing his tunic as he hobbles out*)

DESIREE   Carl-Magnus, what are you doing?

CARL-MAGNUS   My duelling pistols!

    (*And he rushes out.*
        DESIREE *runs after him*)

DESIREE   Carl-Magnus!

    (*The bed rolls off*)

MADAME ARMFELDT   A great deal seems to be going on in this house tonight.

    (*Pause*)

Child, will you do me a favor?

FREDRIKA   Of course, Grandmother.

MADAME ARMFELDT   Will you tell me what it's all for? Having outlived my own illusions by centuries, it would be soothing at least to pretend to share some of yours.

FREDRIKA (*After thought*)   Well, I think it must be worth it.

MADAME ARMFELDT   Why?

FREDRIKA   It's all there is, isn't it? Oh, I know it's often discouraging, and to hope for something too much is childish, because what you want so rarely happens.

A LITTLE NIGHT MUSIC

MADAME ARMFELDT Astounding! When I was your age I
wanted everything—the moon—jewels, yachts, villas on the
Riviera. And I got 'em, too,—for all the good they did me.

(*Music. Her mind starts to wander*)

There was a Croatian Count. He was my first lover. I can
see his face now—such eyes, and a mustache like a brigand.
He gave me a wooden ring.

FREDRIKA A wooden ring?

MADAME ARMFELDT It had been in his family for centuries,
it seemed, but I said to myself: a wooden ring? What sort
of man would give you a wooden ring, so I tossed him out
right there and then. And now—who knows? He might
have been the love of my life.

(*In the* GARDEN, FREDRIK *and* CHARLOTTE *pause*)

CHARLOTTE To think I was actually saying: How I hate you
being happy! It's—as if I carry around some terrible curse.

(CARL-MAGNUS *enters from house, runs down steps*)

Oh, Mr. Egerman . . . I'm sorry.

(CHARLOTTE *breaks from* FREDRIK *with a little cry.*
    FREDRIK, *still dazed, merely turns, gazing vaguely at*
CARL-MAGNUS)

172

CARL-MAGNUS (*Glaring, clicks his heels*)   Sir, you will accompany me to the Pavilion.

(CHARLOTTE *looks at the pistol. Slowly the wonderful truth begins to dawn on her. He really cares! Her face breaks into a radiant smile*)

CHARLOTTE   Carl-Magnus!

CARL-MAGNUS (*Ignoring her*)   I think the situation speaks for itself.

CHARLOTTE (*Her ecstatic smile broadening*)   Carl-Magnus, dear, you won't be *too* impulsive, will you?

CARL-MAGNUS   Whatever the provocation, I remain a civilized man.

(*Flourishing the pistol*)

The lawyer and I are merely going to play a little Russian Roulette.

CHARLOTTE   Russian Roulette?

CARL-MAGNUS (*To* FREDRIK)   Well, sir? Are you ready, sir??

FREDRIK (*Still only half aware*)   I beg your pardon. Ready for what??

A LITTLE NIGHT MUSIC

🖋

CHARLOTTE (*Thrilled*)   Russian Roulette!

FREDRIK   Oh, Russian Roulette. That's with a pistol, isn't it?
And you spin the . . .

> (*Indicating*)

Well, why not?

> (*Very polite, to* CHARLOTTE)

Excuse me, Madame.

> (CARL-MAGNUS *clicks his heels and struts off.* FREDRIK
> *follows him off slowly*)

MR. LINDQUIST (*Sings*)
A weekend in the country . . .

MR. LINDQUIST and MRS. ANDERSSEN
So inactive

MR. LINDQUIST, MRS. ANDERSSEN and MR. ERLANSEN
That one has to lie down.

MR. LINDQUIST, MRS. ANDERSSEN, MR. ERLANSEN, MRS. SEGSTROM, MRS. NORDSTROM
A weekend in the country
Where . . .

> (FRID *and* PETRA *enter, unobserved, and lean against a tree.*
> GUNSHOT)

We're twice as upset as is in town!

> (THE QUINTET *scatters and runs off, except for* MRS. ANDERSSEN *who stands behind a tree.*
> DESIREE *runs out of the house and down to* CHARLOTTE)

DESIREE   What is it? What's happened?

CHARLOTTE   Oh, dear Miss Armfeldt, my husband and Mr. Egerman are duelling in the pavilion!

DESIREE   Are you insane? You let them do it?

> (*She starts to run to the* PAVILION.
> CARL-MAGNUS *enters, carrying* FREDRIK *over one shoulder. Quite roughly, he tosses him down on the grass, where* FREDRIK *remains motionless*)

DESIREE   You lunatic! You've killed him! Fredrik!

175

A LITTLE NIGHT MUSIC

CHARLOTTE Carl-Magnus!

CARL-MAGNUS My dear Miss Armfeldt, he merely grazed his ear. I trust his performance in the Law Courts is a trifle more professional.

> (*He clears his throat.*
>   *To* CHARLOTTE)

I am prepared to forgive you, dear. But I feel this house is no longer a suitable place for us.

CHARLOTTE Oh yes, my darling, I agree!

CARL-MAGNUS You will pack my things and meet me in the stables. I will have the car ready.

CHARLOTTE Yes, dear. Oh, Carl-Magnus! You became a tiger for me!

> (*They kiss*)

MRS. ANDERSSEN (*Sings*)
Men are stupid, men are vain,
Love's disgusting, love's insane,
A humiliating business . . .

MRS. SEGSTROM
Oh, how true!

(CARL-MAGNUS *and* CHARLOTTE *break the kiss.* CARL-MAGNUS *exits.* CHARLOTTE *runs up to the house*)

MRS. ANDERSSEN
Aaaah,

(*When* CHARLOTTE *closes the house doors*)

Well . . .

DESIREE   Fredrik? Fredrik!

FREDRIK (*Stirs, opens his eyes, looks dazedly around*)   I don't suppose this is my heavenly reward, is it?

DESIREE   Hardly, dear, with *me* here.

FREDRIK (*Trying to sit up, failing, remembering*)   Extraordinary, isn't it? To hold a muzzle to one's temple—and yet to miss! A shaky hand, perhaps, is an asset after all.

DESIREE   Does it hurt?

177

FREDRIK It hurts—spiritually. You've heard, I imagine, about the evening's other event?

DESIREE No what?

FREDRIK Henrik and Anne—ran off together.

DESIREE Fredrik!

FREDRIK Well, I think I should get up and confront the world, don't you?

DESIREE (*Sings*)
  Isn't it rich?

FREDRIK (*Sings*)
  Are we a pair?
  You here at last on the ground.

DESIREE
  You in mid-air.

  (*Speaks*)

  Knees wobbly?

178

FREDRIK   No, no, it seems not. In fact, it's hardly possible, but . . .

DESIREE (*Sings*)
Was that a farce?

FREDRIK (*Sings*)
My fault, I fear.

DESIREE
Me as a merry-go-round.

FREDRIK
Me as King Lear.

(*Speaks*)

How unlikely life is! To lose one's son, one's wife, and practically one's life within an hour and yet to feel—relieved. Relieved, and, what's more, considerably less ancient.

(*He jumps up on the bench*)

Aha! Desiree!

DESIREE   Poor Fredrik!

179

⚓

FREDRIK No, no, no. We will banish "poor" from our vocabulary and replace it with "coherent."

DESIREE (*Blank*) Coherent?

FREDRIK Don't you remember your manifesto in the bedroom? A coherent existence after so many years of muddle? You and me, and of course, Fredrika?

(*They kiss. The music swells*)

FREDRIK (*Sings*)
Make way for the clowns.

DESIREE (*Sings*)
Applause for the clowns.

BOTH
They're finally here.

(*The music continues*)

FREDRIK (*Speaks*) How does Malmo appeal to you? It'll be high sunburn season.

DESIREE Why not?

FREDRIK Why not?

DESIREE Oh God!

FREDRIK What is it?

180

DESIREE   I've got to do Hedda for a week in Halsingborg.

FREDRIK   Well, what's wrong with Purgatory before Paradise? I shall sit through all eight performances.

(*They go slowly upstage.*
FREDRIKA *wakes up*)

FREDRIKA   Don't you think you should go to bed, Grandmother?

MADAME ARMFELDT   No, I shall stay awake all night for fear of missing the first cock-crow of morning. It has come to be my only dependable friend.

FREDRIKA   Grandmother—

MADAME ARMFELDT   What, dear?

FREDRIKA   I've watched and watched, but I haven't noticed the night smiling.

MADAME ARMFELDT   Young eyes are not ideal for watching. They stray too much. It has already smiled. Twice.

FREDRIKA   It has? Twice? For the young—and the fools?

MADAME ARMFELDT   The smile for the fools was particularly broad tonight.

181

A LITTLE NIGHT MUSIC

FREDRIKA   So there's only the last to come.

MADAME ARMFELDT   Only the last.

> (MADAME ARMFELDT *dies.*
>
> *We become more aware of the underscoring, the same used under the opening waltz.*
>
> HENRIK *and* ANNE *suddenly waltz on, and then all of the* OTHER COUPLES, *at last with their proper partners, waltz through the scene.*
>
> *The screens close, and* MR. LINDQUIST *appears at the piano. He hits one key of the piano, just as he did at the opening.*
>
> *And the play is over*)